Introductory Note
By Joseph Hansen

This study deals with a subject that to many socialist militants might appear at first sight as hardly of great concern: *What is the first form of government that can be expected to appear as the result of a successful anticapitalist revolution, and how does it relate to the preceding struggle for power?*

The topic itself came under consideration quite late in the development of key revolutionary-socialist concepts. It was submitted for general discussion for the first time at the Fourth Congress of the Communist International in 1922. Only the delegates of the Bolshevik Party, in the period when it was led by Lenin and Trotsky, could have suggested the importance of the question to the cadres of the Third International.

The delegates at the Fourth Congress did not engage in fanciful speculation. Their debate was based on the experience of the October 1917 revolution in Russia, on five years of thinking over that mighty chapter in the development of civilization, and on the need to bring subsequent experiences into the context of the lessons of 1917.

After 1922 the subject was not taken up again. The life-and-death struggle with Stalinism cut across further development of Marxist theory on this question as on much else. Trotsky referred to it in passing in the Transitional Program, which was adopted at the founding congress of the Fourth International in 1938, but he did not enlarge upon it.

The necessity to resume where the Fourth Congress of the Communist International had left off arose from new complex events in the international class struggle. In the aftermath of World War II, workers states appeared in Eastern Europe, China, Korea, Vietnam, and Cuba. The processes through which these states came into being had to be explained correctly in the light of Marxist theory.

Failure to do so would have put in question the continuity of Marxist theory, including Trotsky's analysis of the meaning of the extension of the borders of the Soviet Union at the beginning of World War II and eventually his analysis of the degeneration of the first workers state.

To carry out this task, the significance of the post-World War II overturns of capitalism had to be connected with the conclusions reached by the Fourth Congress in 1922. Those conclusions had to be either rejected, extended, or modified as the facts might dictate.

The importance of the question becomes obvious when it is thought through and the consequences for political practice are grasped. Nonetheless, it is a fact that it remains a field of prime interest only to advanced revolutionary cadres. This holds true for the world Trotskyist movement as a whole.

The main reason for this discounting of the question is to be found, I think, in the paramountcy of problems facing small revolutionary organizations in disseminating a revolutionary-socialist outlook among the masses. A better understanding of what is involved can be gained if we single out three general aspects, or phases, of this consciousness-raising process—not forgetting, of course, that in the final analysis they mesh together:

1. The educational work of bringing the masses to understand that the great social and economic evils they suffer from are consequences of capitalism in its death agony, and that the dilemma facing humanity on a world scale with ever-increasing acuteness is *socialism* or *barbarism*. The task is preeminent in countries where the program of revolutionary socialism is represented by only small minority movements.

2. The organizational work of building a revolutionary-socialist mass party as the means

for meeting the central dilemma. The problem facing small revolutionary groups of linking up with the masses comes under this heading. The task demands doggedness, the utmost attention, and an expenditure of time and effort bordering on fanaticism.

3. The final push of playing a leading role in the working-class struggle for power when the conditions for this have matured.

For periods longer than expected, revolutionists have had to concentrate on the two preliminary phases. The associated tasks are just as difficult as those of the third phase—perhaps more so. The preliminary problems, standing in some instances for years, if not decades, at the top of the revolutionary agenda, can certainly appear to be more real than the question of what form of government might appear as the consequence of a revolutionary victory.

However, in today's highly unstable world, seemingly remote theoretical questions have a way of suddenly imposing themselves in the political arena and demanding answers that can decisively determine the fate of groups and currents bidding for leadership of the working class. Thus problems related to the struggle for power cannot be placed in deep-freeze to be brought out "when the time comes." They are with us now, both in the sense of internationally important events on which stands must be taken (the Cuban victory, for instance), and in the sense of gaining a more concrete appreciation of the possibilities in coming struggles.

Moreover, the struggle for power, along with the accompanying problems and tasks, must be kept constantly in mind. As the goal, that culminating phase dominates our decisions in selecting the means required for its realization.

Bob Chester was one of the cadres of the Socialist Workers Party who saw the importance of studying that feature of a socialist revolution called a "workers and farmers government." He set out to gain an independent understanding of the phenomenon, going back to the Russian experience and moving to subsequent events in other countries.

He had not finished his study when he died of a heart attack on June 22, 1975. The manuscript he left was thus somewhat rough. Perhaps in a final draft he would have dealt with some points at greater length while compressing others or placing them in a different order.

Certainly he would not have changed his views. The more material he gathered and thought over the more convinced he became of the importance of the topic. I am sure he would have felt deep satisfaction if his study succeeded in helping others to gain the insights he achieved through this work even though they might not agree with everything he said or the way he put it.

Robert Chester

Introduction
By Robert Chester

The term "workers and farmers government" has been used in two senses in the revolutionary Marxist movement. First, as a popular designation for the dictatorship of the proletariat established as the result of a revolutionary upheaval against capitalism. Secondly, in a narrower and more accurate sense, as a label for a regime that has broken politically from capitalism but which has not replaced the capitalist state structure by a workers state and which may not reach the point of doing so.

Such a government, the possibilities of which were discussed at the Fourth Congress of the Comintern in 1922 in the light of the experience of the Russian revolution, was viewed by the Bolsheviks as a passing phase.

Its distinguishing characteristic is its independence from the capitalist ruling class, a fact demonstrated by the capacity of such governments to take sweeping measures against capitalist property relations and the capitalist state as a whole.

It stands in contradiction to capitalist property relations, which still remain dominant economically and socially. If such a government, because of hesitation or a class-collaborationist orientation, fails to deal a death blow to capitalism by establishing a workers state, it will face a counterattack and defeat by the bourgeoisie and its allies.

To establish a workers state, a workers and farmers government must mobilize mass support to assault the foundations of capitalist power: breaking up the capitalist repressive forces and bureaucratic command posts; nationalizing industry, transport, banking, and finances; taking control of foreign trade; and laying the groundwork for a planned economy.

The role of a "workers and farmers government" in revolutionary strategy and tactics was developed in some detail at the Fourth Congress of the Communist International in 1922. Various possible forms and roles for such a government were posed at that time. Excerpts from this discussion can be found in the Education for Socialists publication *The Workers and Farmers Government*, by Joseph Hansen.

Following the second world war, workers and farmers governments emerged in Yugoslavia, China, and other countries that won their independence in national liberation struggles. The establishment of a government in opposition to the bourgeoisie was a decisive step in making possible the measures that overturned capitalism in several instances.

Joseph Hansen, who has done pioneering work on this question, pointed to the workers and farmers government as "the link in the revolutionary process through which this qualitative leap was made possible."[1]

These transformations took place in a manner not anticipated by the Marxist movement. They were led by Stalinist parties opposed to revolutionary socialism or by middle-class nationalist formations lacking a revolutionary program. The working class did not play a preeminent role in the leading parties and often were in the background of the mass movements as well, prior to the direct attack on capitalist property.

Yet these leaderships found themselves, out of necessity, taking revolutionary measures and emerging at the head of workers states—deformed, incomplete, devoid of the organs of democratic popular control demanded by Leninist norms. These states nonetheless met the key economic criteria that determine the existence of a workers state—expropriation of the capitalists and conversion of basic industry into publicly owned property. This unexpected historical development calls for an examination of what took place and an analysis of the causes of this new phenomenon.

The key task of our epoch is the establishment of workers states as the basis for building world socialism. The transformations that will be examined here do not conform to what revolutionary Marxists believe will be the main pattern of overthrowing capitalism and achieving workers states, especially in the advanced countries. In each case, these transformations took place under circumstances that made them exceptions to the general historic course. An examination of how they occurred will enable us better to judge what possibilities exist for their repetition. Such an examination will also give us a better understanding of the shifts in world forces that have taken place in the last thirty years.

CHAPTER ONE
HISTORICAL BACKGROUND

In his magnificent work *State and Revolution*, Lenin traces the development of the Marxist concept of the transfer of power. When it was first presented by Marx and Engels in *The Communist Manifesto*, the transition was posed in general terms. The course of the class struggle would be to "raise the proletariat to the position of the ruling class, to win the battle of democracy," and

> the proletariat will use its political supremacy to wrest, by degrees, all capital from the bourgeoisie, to centralise all instruments of production in the hands of the state, i.e., of the proletariat organised as the ruling class; and to increase the total of productive forces as rapidly as possible.[1]

After analyzing the French revolution of 1848, Marx came to the conclusion (presented in *The Eighteenth Brumaire of Louis Bonaparte*) that the working class could not take over the organs of government of the bourgeoisie, but would have to break them up and replace them with its own organs, as well as replace the dictatorship of the bourgeoisie with the dictatorship of the proletariat. How this could be done was demonstrated in life by the Paris Commune, which Marx subjected to careful analysis, later expanded upon by Lenin in *State and Revolution*.

The revolution of 1905 added another vital link with the appearance of soviets, the representative bodies that formulate and carry out the needs of the revolution. To this Lenin added the special role of the mass-based revolutionary combat party, which takes the lead in the revolution and then plays the leading role in effecting the changes necessary to establish the dictatorship of the proletariat and build the workers state.

Trotsky's theoretical contribution, the permanent revolution, analyzed how, even in a backward country that had not yet completed its bourgeois revolution, the aim of the workers and their peasant allies must be the establishment of a dictatorship of the proletariat, with the workers playing the leading role even though they constitute a minority of the population.

In the age of imperialism, Trotsky argued, the major bourgeois-democratic tasks can be achieved only in the course of the socialist revolution, through the establishment of a workers state. This requires the nationalization of the basic means of production, and banking and finance; state control of foreign trade and internal commerce; and the enactment of a broad land-reform program that eliminates the feudal landlords, and breaks the power of the rich peasants and their allies in the countryside. Land may be divided and distributed to the peasants, or the latter may be organized into cooperatives, but the aim would be to set up—when it becomes feasible—a system of state-run farms where the agricultural workers would play a role similar to that of the factory workers. All these steps could be accomplished only through the mass participation of the workers and peasants in deciding their own future in their own interests.

The revolution cannot stop at the national stage. Trotsky wrote:

> The conquest of power by the proletariat does not complete the revolution, but only opens it. Socialist construction is conceivable only on the foundation of the class struggle, on a national and international scale. This struggle, under the conditions of an overwhelming predominance of capitalist

relationships on the world arena, must inevitably lead to explosions, that is, internally to civil wars and externally to revolutionary wars. Therein lies the permanent character of the socialist revolution as such, regardless of whether it is a backward country that is involved, which only yesterday accomplished its democratic revolution, or an old capitalist country which already has behind it a long epoch of democracy and parliamentarism.[2]

The Russian revolution of 1917 proved the validity of Lenin's and Trotsky's contributions. The victory also posed a series of new problems stemming from several causes: the terrible drain of the imperialist war and the civil war that destroyed major parts of the country's industry and railroads; the small size of the cohesive, politically advanced proletariat, which suffered very heavy casualties in the civil war; the backwardness of the huge peasantry, whose illiteracy rate was more than 75 percent; the intervention of the imperialist powers both on the economic plane and in the civil war, which was conducted on twenty different fronts; and the necessity of solving a host of new problems, never before faced in history, which piled in upon the Bolsheviks all at once.

What was the class nature of the new government and the new state? It was characterized as a dictatorship of the proletariat and a workers state from the beginning, since that was the program on which the Bolsheviks came to power. The overturn of capitalism was, moreover, their declared aim, and everyone knew they were determined to achieve it. At first they gave the new government different titles: workers and peasants government, a soviet of workers and poor peasants, a workers state, and a socialist state. These designations most often described aims rather than the current reality. It took a few years before the stages were analyzed with greater precision.

The October Congress of Soviets set up a provisional government of the Council of Peoples Commissars, responsible to the Congress of Soviets and its Central Executive Committee. Three weeks later a socialist coalition of Bolsheviks and Left Social Revolutionaries (SRs), a peasant-based party, was formed. The new All Union Central Executive Committee was composed of 108 representatives from the Soviets of Workers and Soldiers Deputies, 108 from the Peasants Congress, 100 from the army, and 50 from the trade unions.[3] Three SRs were appointed to head commissariats, which they held until differences over the Brest Litovsk treaty with Germany resulted in their resignation. The coalition lasted about six months.

On the economic field, only the first steps were taken to effect the transition. Banks were nationalized. Land was expropriated from the landowners—in most cases by the peasants themselves, among whom it was distributed. The small holdings of working peasants and Cossacks were exempted from confiscation, but the buying and selling of land was prohibited. Control of the distribution of all other lands was in the hands of local self-government organs.

In the factories, workers control through factory committees had become fairly common. A Council on National Economy was set up on December 14, 1917, "to organize the economic activity of the nation and the financial resources of the government."[4] As the historian E.H. Carr puts it, "The more common state of relations between surviving capitalist organs and the instruments of the new power seems to have been an uneasy, distrustful and quasi-hostile cooperation."[5] During the winter of 1917–18, the council gradually established control over the key industrial areas, and nationalizations began.

The capitalists were still a significant factor in economic life. In fact, Lenin characterized the period as "state capitalism": Capitalists could lease enterprises from nationalized industries and could operate enterprises in all non-nationalized areas. At that point Lenin wrote:

> Instead of advancing from partial nationalization to a general socialization of large-scale industry, agreements with 'captains of industry' must lead to the formation of big trusts directed by them and embracing basic industries, which from an outside view may have the appearance of state undertakings. Such a system of organized production creates a social base for the evolution of state

> capitalism and constitutes a transitional stage towards it.[6]

It is clear from this that the dominant economic form was still not nationalized industry.

Lenin wrote in April 1918, "If in approximately six months' time state capitalism became established in our republic, this would be a great success and a sure guarantee that within a year socialism will have gained a permanently firm hold. . . ."[7] Lenin said this in a polemic against Bolsheviks who accused him of instituting "state capitalism."

The aim was to set up a system of nationwide accounting, control of production, and distribution of goods. "The principal difficulty lies in the economic sphere, namely, the introduction of the strictest and universal accounting and control of the production and distribution of goods, raising the productivity of labor and *socialising* production *in practice*."[8] It became apparent fairly early, however, that this would require a considerably longer time than first appeared necessary.

But then a new factor intervened—the civil war. It posed a series of crucial tasks the new government had to meet in order to survive. The army had to be rebuilt from scratch. It had to be supplied from industries that were in a state of collapse. Transportation, particularly the railway system, was, if anything, in a worse state. Famine threatened the countryside. The Bolsheviks survived only by the most draconian measures, putting severe strains on the economy. Capitalist elements that had found it expedient to compromise with the Bolsheviks during the first period now turned to open sabotage and had to be overcome. The period of rapid nationalization and reorganization beginning with July 1918 was part of the general period known as "war communism."

The civil war also heightened the crisis on the political front. The relations with the Left SRs sharpened because of differences over the Brest Litovsk agreement. Then in July came the assassination by a Left SR of the German ambassador, Count Mirbach, followed a month later by an attempt on Lenin's life. These events culminated in the breakdown of the alliance. The SRs resigned from the government and the Bolsheviks now had to rule alone.

It is possible to identify the stages in this transition. In November 1917 the Bolshevik-SR coalition, with the Bolsheviks playing the leading role, set up a workers and farmers government with the aim of overturning the old order as rapidly as possible. Beginning with the reorganization of the disintegrating capitalist economy and the distribution of the land to the peasants, they moved into the transition period of a mixed economy—"state capitalism," as Lenin labeled it. Under the pressure of the civil war, the Bolsheviks were forced to nationalize the factories and basic industry, as well as transport. "War communism" was the name given this period. At the same time, the coalition with the Left SRs broke down.

Thus the regime established by the Bolsheviks carried out the overturn of capitalism. This proved to be a definitive turning point on the economic level. Even after "war communism" was shelved in favor of the "New Economic Policy," 92 percent of industrial production was carried out in nationalized firms, and foreign trade remained a state monopoly.[9]

The Bolshevik regime differed greatly from the "workers and farmers governments" that instituted workers states after the second world war. It was the product of a proletarian upheaval led by a party that was working-class in program and composition. The politically conscious and organized workers controlled the regime through soviets in the initial period. The regime declared its socialist objectives to the world and denounced illusions about the possibility of collaboration with the bourgeoisie.

Under these circumstances, the use of the term "dictatorship of the proletariat" to designate the new government signaled the fact that all its energies were bent toward firmly establishing the workers as the ruling class.

Nonetheless, in his report on the Fourth World Congress of the Communist International in 1922, Trotsky presented the Bolshevik government as an example of a "workers and farmers government" confronting the task of establishing a full-fledged proletarian dictatorship. He stated:

> A moment may arrive when the Communists together with the left elements of the Social Democracy will set up a work-

ers' government in a way similar to ours in Russia when we created a workers' and peasants' government together with the Left Social-Revolutionaries. Such a phase would constitute a transition to the proletarian dictatorship, the full and completed one.[10]

In the year following the Russian Revolution, upheavals took place in several countries of Europe. The German revolution was aborted, and the Communist leaders Luxemburg and Liebknecht were assassinated. In Hungary, with the complete collapse of the Karolyi regime, a combination of Social Democrats and the newly formed Communist Party under Bela Kun moved in to fill the vacuum. Coming to power almost without a struggle, they issued decrees setting up a "soviet republic" patterned, as they thought, on the Russian model, nationalized all enterprises above the retail level, and nationalized the large estates. The latter were turned into collectives, an error that alienated many peasants.

The new Republic of Workers, Soldiers and Peasants Councils lasted 133 days. It had an insufficient base in the masses, who had not been politically prepared for that step. It did not have the organization or the forces needed to resist the bourgeois and feudal elements, who had not really been defeated. The government was overthrown, the two leading parties smashed, and the leadership jailed or exiled.

An upheaval also took place in Bavaria. A combination of independent socialists and Social Democrats took over the government after a series of demonstrations, resulting from the economic crisis, had forced the bourgeois ministers to resign. Elections were held in which the socialist coalition was defeated. A rump section of the coalition then seized power and proclaimed a Soviet Republic. This government was then deposed and replaced with one headed by the new Communist Party. After a few weeks, the white terror instituted by troops sent in by the central government, headed by the Social Democrat Ebert, ended the brief Bavarian Soviet. It had been in power less than a month.

What was the nature of these two governments? Even though they tried to copy it, they were not similar to the Bolshevik-led government in Russia. In reality they were organizations thrown up by the social unrest engendered by World War I and inspired by the example of the Russian Revolution. The parties were immature, with untested leaders and cadres. Their "soviets" were makeshift imitations of the Russian ones, not truly representative bodies supported by the masses of workers, soldiers, and peasants.

But governments must have a class nature. The appearance of these regimes, temporary as they were, plus the growing influence of the Labour Party in Britain and the continued power of the Social Democracy in Germany, induced the Communist International to take a closer look at them.

This examination was made at the Fourth Congress of the Comintern in 1922, where it was the major point of discussion along with the tactic of the united front. The congress's conclusions were issued in the form of a set of theses and tactics. In relation to the united-front tactic the question was asked: What would be the result if a united front were able to win the support of the workers and actually come to power? The following excerpts give the congress' main trend of thought:

> The call for a workers government (eventually a government of the peasants as well) should be raised everywhere as a *general propaganda slogan*....
>
> In these countries, the slogan of a "workers government" is an inevitable consequence of the entire united-front tactic....
>
> In the common struggle of all these workers against the bourgeoisie, the entire state apparatus must fall into the hands of the workers government, and in this way the position of the working class will be strengthened.
>
> The most elementary program of a workers government must consist in arming the proletariat, disarming the counterrevolutionary bourgeois organizations, installing supervision over production, insuring that the main burden of taxation falls on the rich, and smashing the resistance of the bourgeois counterrevolution....
>
> The proletariat's mere attempt to form a workers government will immediately encounter the most violent resistance on the part

of the bourgeoisie. The slogan of a workers government is therefore capable of giving a focus to and setting off revolutionary struggles.[11]

The document takes up five types of workers governments that can result from this tactic. Possibility number three is "A workers and peasants government. This is possible in the Balkans, Czechoslovakia, etc." In discussing the Congress' attitude toward these transitional regimes, the document concludes: "They do not represent a necessary form of transition toward the dictatorship, but they can serve as a point of departure for attaining this dictatorship. The full dictatorship of the proletariat can only be accomplished by a workers government composed of Communists."[12]

Workers governments led by proletarian revolutionists—the only kind of government that could accomplish the proletarian dictatorship, according to the Fourth Congress—did not materialize in the 1920s and 1930s. Instead, the development of Stalinism led to the degeneration of the theory and practice of the Communist International. The Menshevik concept of revolution—holding that bourgeois democracy must be fully achieved before the proletarian revolution can take place—was revived in the form of the "two-stage theory of revolution." The Menshevik practice of participating in coalition governments with the bourgeoisie was revived in the form of a "popular front" which proclaimed the need to unite all classes under a "democratic" regime. This led to a series of defeats beginning with the crushing of the Chinese revolution of 1925–27.

Trotsky fought this degeneration at every point as the leader of the Left Opposition in the Soviet CP and later as leader of the International Left Opposition. When the Stalinized Third International proved incapable of combating Hitler's rise to power in Germany, Trotsky and his adherents decided that a new world party of socialist revolution, the Fourth International, was needed. The founding congress of the Fourth International was held in 1938.

In the main programmatic document adopted by the founding congress, the *Transitional Program*, Trotsky evaluated the likelihood of the development of workers and farmers governments in the light of all these experiences:

> The experience of Russia demonstrated, and the experience of Spain and France once again confirms, that even under very favorable conditions the parties of petty-bourgeois democracy (S.R.'s, Social Democrats, Stalinists, Anarchists) are incapable of creating a government of workers and peasants, that is, a government independent of the bourgeoisie.

Then came an often-quoted paragraph:

> Is the creation of such a government by the traditional workers' organizations possible? Past experience shows, as has already been stated, that this is, to say the least, highly improbable. However, one cannot categorically deny in advance the theoretical possibility that, under the influence of completely exceptional circumstances (war, defeat, financial crash, mass revolutionary pressure, etc.), the petty-bourgeois parties including the Stalinists may go further than they themselves wish along the road to a break with the bourgeoisie. In any case one thing is not to be doubted: even if this highly improbable variant somewhere at some time becomes a reality and the "workers' and farmers' government" in the above-mentioned sense is established in fact, it would represent merely a short episode on the road to the actual dictatorship of the proletariat.[13]

At the time this seemed to close the book on the appearance of such governments. But the second world war and its aftermath provided exceptional conditions of the type Trotsky noted. In several countries, as a result of national liberation struggles, workers and farmers governments came into being. And, in a manner not anticipated by the Bolsheviks, including Trotsky, they ended up establishing workers states.

An examination of the processes and conditions in which these transformations took place will contribute to the understanding of why they took place and whether they require any changes in our theory or tactics.

Four cases will be examined below—Yugoslavia, China, Cuba, and Algeria. In all four countries the leaderships came to power through deepgoing national liberation struggles. In three, the governments carried out the overturn of capitalism. In the fourth, Algeria, the process was aborted and a capitalist state was consolidated.

In Soviet-occupied Eastern Europe the transitions took place under the direct supervision of Stalin and the Soviet Army, and therefore call for a separate study.

CHAPTER TWO
YUGOSLAVIA

Yugoslavia before World War II was a typical Balkan country. Composed of six different nationalities comprising some 16 million people, it was predominantly agricultural (80 percent of the population were peasants) and suffered from the problems of a semicolonial, semifeudal country. Its main economic role was that of supplier of agricultural products and minerals to Europe.

The Karageorgevic dynasty ruled as pawns of foreign capital. Democratic rights were severely restricted and revolutionary parties were banned. Most of the leaders of the underground Yugoslav Communist Party (CPY) had spent time in prison, and in 1936, when Tito took over the leadership—on appointment from the Comintern—the party was in shambles. Under his leadership the party was rebuilt, so that by 1939 it had a membership of 12,000, with a strong working-class component, and a youth section of 30,000. Considering that this represented the cadre and that the party had a broad periphery of sympathizers, the CPY was a considerable force.

When Hitler won control of most of Western Europe in the first year of the war, the government took a pro-Axis orientation. A coup d'état on March 27, 1941, changed this policy, Hitler responded April 6 with a series of devastating bombing attacks and invasion, overrunning the country in a week. The royal government then fled into exile in London. Scattered remnants of the army in Serbia began to carry out guerrilla actions under General Mihajlovic. At the same time, under the leadership of the Communist Party, partisan guerrilla groups began to operate, gradually fusing into a centralized national command under Tito. The partisans had a mass base from the start. They maintained a policy of working with anyone who was willing to fight the Nazis, and they conducted an irreconcilable struggle.

This was a heroic chapter in Yugoslav history, in which the partisans fought and sacrificed against immense odds. Their goal was national liberation and they were strongly antimonarchist in sentiment. Their central slogan was "Death to the fascists, liberty to the people." They had a pro-Soviet orientation and identified their struggle against the Nazis with that of the Soviet army.

Conflict between the partisans and the Mihajlovic forces developed quickly. Mihajlovic considered himself a representative of the royal government and insisted that the partisans subordinate themselves to him. However, since they had broader forces and the support of larger sections of the population, the partisans insisted on equality and joint actions. Negotiations broke down and each organization operated independently.

In the competition that followed, the social reforms advocated by the partisans and their promise to build a democratically based government won them a dominant position. Mihajlovic, operating on the level of a royalist army officer, was never able to build a significant following and soon began to concentrate more of his military activity against the partisans than against the Nazis. As the war continued, the Mihajlovic forces progressively degenerated, sometimes aiding the Nazis in attacks on the partisans.

The Allies, however, including Stalin, favored Mihajlovic and built him up as an international hero, while the work of the partisans was either ignored or attributed to Mihajlovic, who received all the Allied supplies until the last stages of the war. The partisans had to supply themselves from the population and from captured enemy equipment. Wherever they controlled an area, the partisans set up elections for "people's committees," which took over all functions of government as well as of defense. Stalin looked askance at these indigenous formations and withheld supplies and other aid while he tried to force Tito to join forces with Mihajlovic.

As the partisans broadened their activity and spread into other areas, a national military organization was established. Parallel with this an Anti-Fascist Council of People's Liberation (AVNOJ) was set up in November 1942 by delegates of the local people's committees. This was done without the approval of Stalin or the Allies, who were then meeting at Tehran. Dedijer, in his biography of Tito, says that AVNOJ originally intended to elect a provisional government but gave up the idea as a result of pressure from Moscow.[1] Tito is quoted as saying, "This is not the moment for us to form a new Government in the full sense of the word. The international situation is not ripe yet for that."[2]

While Tito and the CPY declared themselves generally in favor of socialism, the question of achieving it was put off for the distant future. In November 1943 the Second Session of the AVNOJ was convened and did set itself up as a provisional government, appointing a temporary cabinet with Tito at its head proclaiming that Yugoslavia would be a federated multinational state. Its form—republic or monarchy—was to be decided after the war.

Of central interest to the Allies was whether Tito intended to introduce some form of communism in Yugoslavia. When Tito met with Churchill in Italy on August 12, 1944, Churchill asked, in his sly way, "Is it not true that there is a large portion of the Serb peasantry who would not be very glad to see the Communist system introduced?"

Tito replied, "We do not intend to impose any such system. I have often stated this publicly."

In response to further questioning, Tito stated succinctly, "We recognise only two classes of Yugoslavs—Quislings and patriots."[3]

At another time he stated, "I am rather concerned by all the questions which are constantly being asked about Communism in Yugoslavia. I have stated quite categorically that we don't intend to introduce it."[4]

Speaking at the second session of the AVNOJ in November 1943, Tito drove this point home. "We have been slandered, and we are still being slandered. All the occupiers and quislings . . . have said (and still say) that our People's Liberation struggle in Yugoslavia is purely a Communist affair: Bolshevization of the country, an attempt by Communists to seize power, the abolition of private property and the destruction of the church and religion, the destruction of culture, and so on and so forth. These slanders are old and threadbare. They have their origin in Goebbels' kitchen. . . ."[5]

The main base of the partisan army was the peasantry, who operated out of their villages, bringing supplies and intelligence, hiding members from the Nazis, caring for the sick and wounded. The core of the army, the shock troops, were the "proletarian brigades" composed largely of workers recruited from the cities. The partisans harassed the Nazi armies and disrupted their supplies, pinning down twenty-five German divisions. In an attempt to overcome this unexpected obstacle, Hitler launched three major offensives that almost succeeded in wiping out Tito's forces. The partisans, however, rallied continually, finally winning important victories against the Germans. At that stage the Allies decided to aid Tito and abandon Mihajlovic. By the end of the war, Tito had a full-fledged army and held undisputed control of the country.

The partisans could not comprehend that the reasons for Stalin's hostility lay in the very same factors that had built their strength. They had fought under their own power and had a broad, independent base in the working class, the peasantry, and large sections of the middle class and in the national movements. Although the Soviet struggle against the Nazi invaders was an inspiration, most of the Yugoslav victories had been achieved without direct Russian aid, even though the partisans had expected it. Thus they developed a fiercely independent power, which Stalin distrusted and sought to undermine.

At Yalta, Stalin agreed to include Yugoslavia in the British sphere of influence. When the war ended, Churchill tried to cash in on Stalin's promise—only to meet the determined resistance of the Yugoslavs. Churchill wanted to return King Peter to the throne, but Tito refused—pointblank. He had bitterly fought Peter's representative, Mihajlovic, and was not now ready to accept Peter. It was only after considerable pressure that the Yugoslavs accepted a compromise agreement for a joint government responsible, not to the king, but to a regency whose members would be approved by the national committee of the AVNOJ. AVNOJ would have full legislative powers until a constituent assembly would make all final decisions.

The new government, sometimes called the Tito-Subasic government, was set up March 7, 1945. Ivan Subasic, the prime minister of the royal government-in-exile in London, represented the interests of the landed nobility and the bourgeoisie. Four other representatives of these "democratic elements" were included in the cabinet. It soon became apparent that none of them had any real base in the population. Control was essentially in the hands of the Communist Party, the leading force in the AVNOJ.

The government faced overwhelming problems. About 1.7 million people had been killed during the war, almost 11 percent of the population. Nazi bombing and shelling had leveled hundreds of towns and villages, as well as major parts of the big cities. Industry and railway lines were wrecked, livestock destroyed, farms ravaged, and the economy was in danger of collapse. Famine threatened the population and emergency measures were required.

One of the first steps was to enact a land reform. The estates of large landowners were redistributed to the peasants. A million acres of land deserted during the war was also redistributed, one-half to individuals and one-half to state farms. A law was passed limiting each holding to sixty acres. Land could no longer be bought or sold without the permission of the "people's authorities," that is, the local or national governing body.

During the war, the AVNOJ had made it a policy to expropriate the factories or establishments of collaborators. This also applied to foreign-owned establishments that collaborated with the Nazis, so that by 1945, after the new government had been set up, 55 percent of industry was already in state hands. In addition, 27 percent of industry was sequestered, that is, placed under state administration; for all practical purposes, this was the same as nationalization. Thus, as Boris Kidric says, "the first manifestation of the socialist nature of our economy did not follow from *formal nationalization* but from the *confiscation of the property of national traitors.*"[6] (Emphasis in original.)

These steps, of course did not sit well with the bourgeois members of the coalition, but they were powerless to do anything about it. Three members resigned after a few months. One of them, Milan Grol, attempted to publish an opposition newspaper. He charged that the government withheld newsprint, that the police confiscated some issues, and that he was forced to close down. He charged the government with a perpetual trial of "delinquents" that eliminated all opposition to the government, and maintained that the CPY refused to share its power with other parties.

It is true that Tito's secret police, the OZNA, kept a tight check on all oppositionists and potential oppositionists. The CPY, trained in the school of Stalinism, followed many of Stalin's methods of political control. This applied to those standing to the left of the CPY as well as to the right. The fact remains that the CPY had undisputed leadership and authority in the country as a result of its wartime record.

Subasic finally resigned, charging that the CPY so dominated the pre-election period for the constituent assembly that a fair vote was not possible. The bourgeois parties decided to boycott the elections, which took place November 11, 1945. The new Federal People's Republic was installed on November 29, and the new constitution was adopted on January 31, 1946.

Tito says of this period,

> We were unable, during the term of office of the unified government, to make any concessions to those elements in the government that were in fact representing the interests of the discarded monarchy, the bourgeoisie and their patrons abroad, in other words international reaction. During the term of office of the unified government, that is while Subasic, Sutej and Grol were in it, we were subjected to great pressure from the Western allies. Impossible concessions were sought for the bourgeois class in Yugoslavia: consistent demands were made for certain rights of the Western democratic kind, which would in effect have meant making it possible for the bourgeoisie in Yugoslavia to instigate a civil war.[7]

The year 1945 thus became the critical year for the CPY leadership. If the concession made on the composition of the government had been followed by further significant concessions, the way would have been opened for the Western powers and their Yugoslav bourgeois-feudal vassals to roll back the advances made during the war. In this the procapitalist forces could have counted on the support of Stalin prior to the outbreak of the cold war.

A similar situation in Greece followed precisely along that path, as a result of the concessions made by the Greek partisan movement to Churchill. A popular uprising brought the CP-led partisans to power in 1944. They permitted the entry of British troops into the country in October. The imperialist forces launched an all-out assault on the workers and peasants. The lessons of this defeat were not lost on the Yugoslav leaders. The independence gained in the wartime struggles, the hatred felt for the old regime, and the pressure exerted by the masses would have made such concessions highly risky for Tito in any case. Moreover, the treatment the CPY forces received during the war made them distrustful both of Stalin and the Western powers. The determination of the CPY leaders to defend what they had won made the next steps inevitable.

The power of the capitalist class and the feudal aristocracy was broken, their economic base deeply eroded, and their control over the economic life of the country curtailed. The new constitution did not eliminate private property or private enterprise. Instead, it provided for three types of economic activity: state, private, and cooperative. (In the latter type, individuals pooled their inventories, which would then be matched by the government, could bid for government contracts.) On the land, although private ownership predominated, there was a small but growing sector of state and cooperative farms.

What type of government was it? All the Yugoslav leaders stressed that their aim was to make Yugoslavia an independent, democratic, federated republic. It was designated a popular-front government or a people's front, which, in Tito's words, "is not only an alliance of workers and peasants; it is something more. It is an alliance of all patriots, all the progressive people of our country, all those who set out on the new road of building and consolidating new Yugoslavia. It is and must remain an alliance of the working people—workers, peasants, the people's intelligentsia, and the remaining working citizens of our country."[8] This was a broad definition, which left the class nature of the government still undefined.

It is possible here to make a more precise definition. A government in which the power of the old ruling classes has been broken, in which their participation in the government has been eliminated, in which the armed forces and police of the old regime have been wiped out, and in which a process of land reform and nationalization of industry is proceeding—such a government has the characteristics of a workers and peasants government. There can be some dispute as to exactly when such a government came into being since the CPY had the real power even during the war.

However, the presence of bourgeois ministers in the government, representing the significant forces of the old regime and seeking to defend bourgeois interests within the new administration, was not an insignificant factor. It had added importance since their presence reflected the terms of international agreements—Yalta and Potsdam—by which the great powers attempted to guarantee the survival of capitalism and a bourgeois government in Yugoslavia. As long as Tito made an effort to remain within the terms of these international agreements, the road towards a socialist revolution was blocked, and the regime's political independence from the bourgeoisie could not be regarded as fully accomplished.

The clearest sign that the Yugoslav CP was not going to be tied down by the Yalta and Potsdam agreements came with the resignation of Subasic, the last and most important of the capitalist watchdogs in the cabinet. The formation of the People's Republic, which gave juridical legitimacy to the radical measures that had been taken, placed the seal on this shift. It is therefore sounder to date the formation of the workers and peasants government from this turning point, rather than an earlier date.

Perhaps the clearest official statement designating this stage was made by Mosa Pijade, the CPY's most important theoretician. "It is not a liberal bourgeois democratic republic," he maintained, "but neither is it a socialist republic. The People's Republic is a higher form of republic than the bourgeois democratic form, but lower than the socialist form."[9]

During the latter part of 1945 and the early part of 1946, sharp disputes took place within the CPY and the government over the proper method of developing the economy. The differences were expressed in the two lines that were counterposed: state capitalism versus state enterprises. The main advocate of the state capitalist approach was Andrija Hebrang, chairman of the Economic Council and minister of industry. He held that the quickest way to complete the reconstruction of the country was through working out arrangements for capitalists to participate in the economic and industrial process. After a period of conflict, he was overruled and removed from his posts.

From early 1946 the main direction was toward building state enterprises and broadening government intervention into all phases of Yugoslav life. The state machinery of management and control went through reorganization—the institution of more thorough financial controls, and state regulation of banking, price structure, and foreign trade. These steps pointed toward establishing a workers state. In addition, the process of planning for industry was begun, and to that end Boris Kidric was sent to Moscow to study Soviet planning. On his return, a Yugoslav five-year plan, aimed at rapid expansion of the industrial sector, was drawn up and inaugurated in April 1947.

The nationalization law of December 1946 prepared the ground for a strong move to take over all industry.

Boris Kidric later told the fifth congress of the CPY:

> It is characteristic of the second period [beginning in the second half of 1946, according to Kidric] that the revolutionary economic measures were already shedding the form they had taken during the Liberation War and were taking on purely socialist forms. The basic outlines of the socialist organization of the state sector of our economy, of its machinery and method of operation were set. . . .
>
> At the start and close of this period, the National Assembly enacted two nationalization laws the result of which was that the whole of industry, mining, wholesale trade, transport, etc., entered the socialist sector of our economy.[10]

In addition to nationalizing native industry, the government also took over foreign holdings. These included mining, metallurgy, metals processing, ceramics, timber, textiles, paper and leather manufacturing.

The changes in internal trade are shown in the following figures. State retail shops grew from 692 in 1945 to 2,391 in 1946 and then to 7,125 in 1948. Cooperative shops rose from 3,716 in 1945 to 10,734 in 1946 and to 16,235 in 1948. In contrast, private shops grew slightly from 35,216 in 1945 to 40,167 in 1946 and dropped to 19,560 in 1948. Total retail trade in private shops dropped from 85 percent in 1945 to 48.8 percent in 1946.

In agriculture, the Yugoslav leadership consciously avoided the pitfalls of Stalin's agricultural policies. The main achievement of the first stage in 1945–46 was the distribution of the land to needy peasants and the limitation of the size of individual holdings. Cooperative and state farms were set up on a limited scale at first, and then expanded in number at a slow rate. The pace of economic transformation on the land, therefore, lagged considerably behind that of the industrial sector.

The process of reorganization and nationalization took place without any serious opposition. This was largely a result of the sharp polarization that occurred during the war and in the immediate postwar period, when it was almost impossible to stay neutral. Most of the royalists either escaped with the government or went over to the Nazis and left the country when the latter were defeated. The national bourgeoisie split into pro-Nazi, pro-Mihajlovic, and even pro-Tito groupings.

As a class it had little power in the postwar period, relying primarily on international pressures to salvage its positions. When this failed some decided to tolerate the new order. In a 1952 conversation with delegates of the Socialist Party of India, Tito pointed out that "not uncommonly in Yugoslavia, the former owner of a nationalized factory works today as a manager, engineer or clerk in his old firm or in a similar enterprise."[11]

Another sign of the transformation that had taken place was the declarations of "socialist" objectives that began to appear in statements of the leaders. These statements first appeared late in 1946 and became general with the announcement of the five-year plan in 1947. The plan set as its objectives the consolidation of Yugoslavia's economic independence, elimination of the effects of its semicolonial past, development of its productive forces and the productivity of labor, and the development of modern techniques in agriculture.

We can conclude that the effective nationalization of industry, the elimination of foreign holdings, the progressive increase in state control of commerce and retail trade, plus the introduction of planning, establish that the point of qualitative change in taking Yugoslavia's economy out of the orbit of capitalism was the implementation and extension of the December 1946 nationalizations.

International developments, of course, played an important part in the process. The opening of the cold war in 1946, carrying with it the growing threat of imperialist intervention, made it all the more necessary to consolidate the economy and the regime. In addition, the growing frictions with Stalin, which culminated in the 1948 split, pressed the Yugoslavs to firm up their political and social base.

The ideology of the Yugoslav leaders was basically nationalist rather than internationalist. They claimed that Yugoslavia could arrive at socialism by its own national path, similar in essence to the "socialism in one country" established in the Soviet Union under Stalin, although different in form. They expanded Stalin's theory to include the achievement of socialism in several countries through independent national routes.

The Tito regime participated in the Cominform (Communist Information Bureau) where, at first, they were hailed by Stalin as a model for East European regimes that were hesitating to break with bourgeois allies in the face of the cold war. Belgrade was the first Cominform headquarters.

However, the Yugoslav leaders related to the other East European regimes as separate national powers, not as part of a unified international movement. Treaties were signed with each state declaring "friendship and close cooperation between the people of both countries and of all the United Nations."[12]

The desire for greater independence from the Soviet leaders and quicker economic development led Tito to raise with some of the East European leaders the idea of forming a Balkan-Danube federation. This helped spur Stalin to break with Tito and launch an all-out effort to isolate and break Yugoslavia. All leaders in Eastern Europe suspected of entertaining ideas about independence were framed-up and shot or jailed. Tito soon dropped the proposal to form a Balkan-Danube federation in favor of closer ties with the capitalist West.

The CPY leaders were all trained in the school of Stalinism and patterned their political structure, as well as the country's economic structure, on that of the Soviet Union. Democracy within the party was limited to discussing how to carry out policies set by the leadership. Up to the point of the break, Stalin was idealized along with Lenin as the fount of Marxism-Leninism. Opposition tendencies were not allowed to function, and dissidents soon found themselves under investigation by the OZNA—the secret police. (This, too, followed a Russian model with which Tito was familiar—the NKVD.)

The same pattern was carried out within the government, where decisions of the party automatically became government policy. Department officers were appointed, as were factory managers, managers of collective farms, etc. Bureaucratic tendencies, which are inevitable in an underdeveloped country in the absence of massive economic aid, grew in a rank way. Elections followed the Kremlin pattern of single slates drawn up by the party. Because of the wartime experiences, the relationship between the CPY leadership and the masses was closer than in the Soviet Union, but the differences were quantitative rather than qualitative. This relationship, however, played an important role during the fight with Stalin, when the ranks of the party and the masses of the country rallied to the defense of Tito.

As a result of these factors, the development of the workers state did not follow the pattern of the early period of the Soviet Union under Lenin. Yugoslavia never experienced the soviet democracy that existed under Lenin. The Yugoslav revolution was deformed by the Stalinist course of the CPY, and the resulting workers state must be designated as deformed. This characterization has stood the test of events. It holds true for Yugoslavia today. In summary, after winning military victories against the Nazis and the forces of Mihajlovic, the Titoists established a workers and peasants government with the elimination of Subasic from the government in October 1945 and the installation of the Federal Peoples Republic. This government proceeded to nationalize industry, regulate banking, and establish a monopoly of foreign trade. It projected an economic plan and proclaimed a socialist orientation. With the implementation and extension of the thoroughgoing nationalizations decreed at the end of 1946, a workers state was established in Yugoslavia.

CHAPTER THREE
CHINA

The new relationship of forces that emerged from the second world war prepared the ground for the revolutionary victory in China in 1949. Chiang Kai-shek's political base steadily narrowed because of the repressive measures taken by his regime and its incapacity to counter the Japanese occupation; while the peasant armies headed by the Chinese Communist Party (CCP), gained control of significant portions of China through their struggle against the Japanese invaders. The changed situation led to a complicated series of maneuvers between the two forces.

The base of China's economy was the exploited peasantry. Their crops were taxed as much as 60 percent by the landlords. They were saddled with all kinds of special taxes, gouged by usurers, raided and ravished in turn by the landlords, the warlords, and the Japanese. Male peasants were always in danger of being drafted into Chiang's army, unless they were able to buy their way out. Once drafted, they were abused, underfed, and otherwise mistreated, so that they died by the thousands. They saw no reason to fight and occupied themselves with the problem of survival.

The Chinese masses had strong anti-Japanese sentiments, especially in the northern border areas adjoining the Japanese-held territory. The sentiment was expressed in the formation of numerous self-defense guerrilla groups, which the military forces under CCP direction were able to coordinate and direct. It was able to advance the struggle into the whole northern area; then, toward the end of the war, it extended its influence into the strategic coastal zone. Wherever Mao's army consolidated its power, it was able to set up governing bodies that made local laws, collected taxes, maintained communications, issued currency, and administered justice.

Landlords' properties were not generally confiscated; instead the emphasis was placed on reduction of rents and interest. A substantial reduction in the percentage of the crop allocated to the landlords won peasant backing for the CCP.

By the end of the war, the liberated areas (or Border Regions as they were officially called) embraced about 95. 5 million people, around one-seventh of the population. The army counted 910,000 in its ranks, with an additional 2.3 million in the militia. Membership in the Chinese Communist Party had risen to 1.2 million. CCP members were thoroughly integrated into the army and governing bodies, and had the respect of the population.

The CCP forces had become expert in combining guerrilla actions with regular operations. It was an all-volunteer army. It did not steal or confiscate its supplies from the peasants, as did Chiang's forces, but paid for its supplies. Soldiers would aid in bringing in the crops or would help in emergencies. They built up strength from their own resources, obtaining arms from combat with the Japanese or the nationalists; they received little help from the Russians or the Americans. Their morale was exceptionally high. They could strike behind Japanese lines and then disappear into hidden bases. Integrated as they were with the population, their intelligence was highly effective.

Taking the best elements from the guerrilla forces and the regular army troops, the Red Army trained them at area schools in military tactics and strategy, and gave them a political indoctrination. After that, they were sent back to fill leadership posts in the armed forces or local governing bodies. The central army school and political center was in Yenan, Mao's headquarters.

The regime in the liberated areas during the war was essentially a CCP-Liberation Army government ruling over an agrarian economy. With eighteen different liberated areas in 1944, Yenan was not able to maintain tight control over local governments, leaving them with considerable autonomy. Village defense groups were integrated into larger bodies for specific actions, after which they returned to their villages. The army was the unifying force and administrative arm of the government, coordinating policies, raising funds and supplies as well as carrying out other administrative duties.

The central stated objectives of the war years were "the defeat of the Japanese aggressors in co-ordination with the allied countries" and the establishment of a "democratic coalition government."[1] Standard practice was to elect local government officials by the "three-thirds system"—that is, allotting one-third of the seats in the councils to the Communist Party, one-third to "progressive elements," and one-third to the "middle class."[2] Since the CCP was the controlling force, however, its proposals took precedence.

The CCP followed the two-stage theory of Stalinism. In his article "On New Democracy" (1940), Mao stated:

> In the historical course of the Chinese revolution two steps must be taken: first, the democratic revolution, and secondly, the socialist revolution; these two revolutionary processes are different in character. [More specifically, Mao said:] The first step is to change a society that is colonial, semi-colonial and semi-feudal into an independent, democratic society. The second is to develop the revolution further and build up a socialist society. In the present Chinese revolution, we are taking the first step.[3]

While giving lip service to socialism as a long-range goal, this policy meant seeking collaboration with bourgeois forces to establish and preserve a reformist capitalist regime.

In the final week of the second world war, Soviet forces invaded Manchuria, and the Japanese surrendered to them. A contest then developed between the CCP-led armies and Chiang's nationalist forces over who would occupy Manchuria, the main industrial center of China. With the support of the U. S. Air Force, Chiang was able to send his best troops into the major cities, while the peasant armies took control of the countryside.

Abiding by the agreements made by Stalin at Yalta, Mao proposed to participate in a bourgeois coalition government to be headed by Chiang, and postpone expropriation of the landlords indefinitely. As a good-will gesture to Chiang, Communist Party forces were withdrawn from eight liberated zones.

Considering Chiang's situation to be untenable, U. S. Ambassador Hurley pressured him into attending a peace conference with Mao. With a U. S. guarantee of safety, Mao was flown by the U. S. Air Force to Chungking on August 28, 1945, for negotiations and a truce agreement. It was finally agreed that the CCP would recognize the Kuomintang as the dominant party in the leadership of the new government, in which the CCP would participate. Both sides would abide by the three principles of Sun Yat-sen, the founder of the Kuomintang. The army would be under Chiang's command, while Chiang would recognize CCP control over twenty divisions.

The three principles of Sun Yat-sen were directed at completing the national bourgeois revolution. The first principle, the Doctrine of Nationalism, was to restore the independence of China from foreign imperialism and establish self-determination of all races in a United Republic. The second principle, the Doctrine of Democracy, would be introduced by stages. The third principle, the Doctrine of Livelihood, included "equalization of the land"—to be accomplished by government regulation of ownership and government collection of the land tax. Redistribution would be achieved through government buying of land from its owners. Finally:

> Enterprises, whether Chinese-owned or foreign owned, which are either monopolistic in character or of a very large scale and cannot be managed by private interests such as banks, railways, air communications, etc., shall be operated and managed by the state, so that private capital cannot hold in its grasp the livelihood of the people; this is the main principle of the control of capital.[4]

While formal agreement existed between Chiang and Mao concerning the program of a coalition regime, the question of the Communist Party's future role was a stumbling block. Chiang insisted that control be concentrated in the central government. He demanded power to appoint or replace any local official. The CCP insisted on its right to control the provincial administrations in the regions it occupied, where, it claimed, officials had been elected by popular vote. The CCP also demanded that Communists be appointed vice-mayors to serve as deputies to Kuomintang-appointed mayors in the major cities. Chiang refused, and further insisted on a majority in the governing bodies sufficient to permit him to ban the CCP, if he so desired. Without sufficient guarantees for its survival as a political force, the CCP would not put itself in a position where it would be at the mercy of the Kuomintang. By October 1945, negotiations had reached a stalemate.

Chiang utilized the truce to transport his best troops to the key Peking-Tientsin area. Equipped with the latest American arms and backed by U. S. air power and Marine combat corps, it was a potent force. After harassing the CP-controlled areas for several months, Chiang opened full-scale hostilities in July 1946, and military conflicts continued sporadically the rest of the year.

During the same period, Chiang consolidated his hold on the main cities of the eastern seaboard. Mass movements of workers and students had begun to arise in these areas, with the workers moving to organize unions and improve wages and working conditions, and with the students demonstrating for peace, democratic rights, and an end to persecution by the Kuomintang. Capitalizing on its wartime military victories, the CCP began to attract followers in the cities. Owing in part to the CCP policy of conciliating Chiang at this time, "the movements were suppressed by the Kuomintang striking blow after blow, until in 1947, generally speaking, the worker and student movements in the great cities were obviously ebbing."[5]

During the same period, peasant pressure for land reform was mounting, especially in the areas under control of the CCP. In July 1946, the party announced a limited land reform, as part of its preparation for a struggle with Chiang. The land-reform movement began to spread rapidly, adding to the pressures.

At the end of 1946, when all preparations were completed, Chiang's government openly barred all the doors to compromise and peace parlies by holding its own "national assembly" and organizing its own "Constituent Government," which showed its determination to eradicate the establishment of any "coalition government" with the CCP. Following these steps, it mobilized a great military offensive (such as the seizure of Chan-Chia-Kow and some small cities and towns in North Kiangsu). Yet up to this moment the CCP had not given up its efforts at conciliation. Its delegates to the peace conference still lingered in Shanghai and Nanking, trying to reopen peace parlies with the Kuomintang through the mediation of the so-called "Third Force"— the "Democratic League."[6]

But Chiang's pressure continued to mount. He opened an offensive that forced the peasant armies (now called the People's Liberation Army [PLA]) to retreat. Chiang even occupied the CCP's former capital at Yenan. The PLA counterattacked in Manchuria. In June 1947, Chiang issued a warrant for the arrest of Mao. This was done in spite of the efforts of General Marshall to obtain a new truce— efforts that repeatedly appeared to be successful, only to be vetoed each time by Chiang.

In 1947, Washington and the other Western powers intensified the cold war, a development that was undoubtedly a factor in Chiang's calculations. It had the additional effect of reducing pressure by Stalin on Mao to find a modus vivendi with Chiang. This, plus the outbreak of the civil war, finally resulted in a left turn. On October 18 the People's Liberation Army issued a manifesto calling for the overthrow of Chiang and the building of a "New China." At the same time the CCP proclaimed a new agrarian law calling for widespread land reform. The civil war now opened in earnest.

Chiang depended on U. S. aid; but the utilization of American troops had become impossible because of the refusal of the GIs to stay abroad. The "Bring Us Home" movement compelled Washington to demobilize its conscript army.

Even though Chiang's army outnumbered the CCP armies and outclassed them in the amount and quality of its arms, Chiang was not in a good position to carry on large-scale warfare. China's economy was approaching collapse—the result of the avaricious appetite of the ruling clique. "With the triumphal Nationalist return to East China . . . restraints were left behind. The restoration of Nationalist rule over Japanese-occupied territory was accompanied by one of the biggest carpet-bagging operations in history."[7] The top leaders and generals seized whatever they could of the Japanese enterprises, took over the main enterprises of the country, and funneled huge quantities of U. S. aid into their own pockets. They looted Formosa (Taiwan), taking over the government and businesses, fleecing the native population by all the methods they had so artfully developed on the mainland.

By July 1946, the economic situation had begun to deteriorate, with inflation rising to runaway proportions. Foreign exchange reserves declined radically as did internal trade and commerce. As a result, sections of the bourgeoisie, especially the lower ranks, began to lose interest in supporting Chiang's military objectives, and moved increasingly toward favoring peace with Mao's forces.

Even though it was considerably smaller, Mao's army was in a position to fight effectively. It was now supplied with arms taken from the Japanese by the Russians. Its forces were well trained in both guerrilla and positional war. It had an experienced and unified leadership, excellent morale, and—as a result of its turn toward land reform—the enthusiastic support of masses of peasants in motion.

As Belden points out:

> The Communist land policy was decisive in the struggle for power in China because it brought hitherto apathetic masses into open revolt against existing society. . . . On the spiritual side, the land reform gave to the peasant one emotion that had perhaps hitherto been lacking from his life—hope. On the more material side, the Communist land reform gave to the peasant a method of struggle against his village rulers.[8]

This movement, setting the peasant against the landlord and his allies, the usurers and government officials, and raising the peasant women to fight against their ancient system of bondage, struck at the roots of Chiang's economic base. Once it began, it spread like a wave throughout the liberated areas and beyond. The PLA surged forward on this wave.

By the end of 1947, Chiang's position in Manchuria became tenuous. Moving into positional warfare, the PLA began to chop up the Nationalist armies, and by the middle of 1948, it had them bottled up. Large sections of Chiang's armies began to desert—with their arms and sometimes with their officers. By the end of the year, Chiang had lost control of Manchuria. He also lost the showdown battle of Hwai-Hai, where huge amounts of American equipment were captured. The remaining nationalist forces retreated in confusion on a broad front. At about this time the United States discontinued its military aid, considering Chiang's position hopeless.

These defeats signaled the end of Chiang's rule. The economic situation became abysmal, and by January 1949 Chiang was forced to resign as president. Negotiations with the CCP failed, and beginning in April the PLA launched a new offensive. The Nationalist forces collapsed before it, and with them the Kuomintang government. The country was thus left with a power vacuum; the PLA and the CCP moved rapidly to fill it.

From these events it becomes clear that the victory of the CCP was not a result of its program or sustained policy, but of a specific series of conditions that enabled it to take power:

1. The Japanese invasion and the second world war, which enabled Mao to build a mass base for an extended period of time;

2. The adamant refusal by Chiang to form a coalition, despite Mao's willingness to subordinate the CCP to the Nationalists;

3. Chiang's decision to force a military showdown, even while his political and economic base was disintegrating;

4. The windfall of arms and munitions from the Japanese that enabled the CCP to conduct large-scale warfare;

5. The tremendous impetus to the liberation movement given by the land reform;

6. The opening of the cold war, which helped spur a left turn by the CCP;

7. The collapse and defeat of Chiang's forces together with the withdrawal of U. S. support, which

led to a power vacuum and permitted the CCP to march into the major cities without a struggle.

The victory represented the triumph of a movement that was essentially peasant rather than proletarian, leaving the ultimate fate of the capitalist social order undecided. Discouraged by the CCP from strikes or other indications of active support for the CCP forces in the last days of Chiang's regime, the city workers lined the streets to greet the People's Liberation Army as it marched in to take command in the cities. The urban masses, by and large, did not participate in the transfer of power.

In the last months of battle, when victory began to seem assured, Mao began to retreat once again on the issue of land reform, although this process was never completely halted as it had been during the second world war. After the cities were occupied, factory owners were instructed to continue production and their property rights were guaranteed. Strikes were barred and other forms of protest were strictly limited. The Communist Party sought to act as the arbiter in all social questions and struggles.

In September 1949 a People's Political Consultative Conference met to ratify an Organic Law and a Central People's Government to provide interim rule. On October 1, a new Chinese People's Republic was formally established. Its flag contained four stars symbolizing the "bloc" of the working class, peasantry, national bourgeoisie, and urban middle classes.

The first article of the Common Program adopted by the conference showed that the regime viewed itself as a coalition formation representing various classes:

> The People's Republic of China is a New Democratic or a People's Democratic state. It carries out the people's democratic dictatorship led by the working class, based on the alliance of workers and peasants, and uniting all democratic classes and all nationalities in China. It opposes imperialism, feudalism and bureaucratic capitalism and strives for independence, democracy, peace, unity, prosperity and strength of China.[9]

The practice of the regime indicated what was intended by this formula: to accomplish the bourgeois democratic revolution in alliance with the bourgeoisie.

In addition to the CCP, the coalition government included the Democratic League of China, a middle-class liberal party that had been banned by Chiang, and the Revolutionary Committee of the Kuomintang, "primarily a regrouping of generals in Southern China who deserted Chiang Kai-shek [and who] must be considered as representing the interests of a section of the Chinese bourgeoisie of the South."[10] Two out of five vice-chairpeople of the government were members of the bourgeoisie.

Mao now claimed to have achieved the aims set down by Sun Yat-sen.

> Except for the question of who is to lead whom, the Kuomintang Principle of Popular Rights [Sun Yat-sen's Principle of Democracy] referred to here, when viewed as a general political program, corresponds to the people's democracy or New Democracy that we have been talking about.[11]

Mao also made clear the attitude of the CCP to the national bourgeoisie.

> ... it is estimated on the basis of certain data that modern industry occupies only about ten percent of the total production of the entire national economy. In order to offset imperialist pressure and to push her backward economy a step forward, China must utilize all elements of urban and rural capitalism which are beneficial and not harmful to the national economy and the people's livelihood.[12]

"Bureaucratic capital," the holdings of Chiang's clique, comprising almost 70 percent of industrial capital, was taken over without compensation. Private enterprises continued to function, but under stricter government supervision.

> In Private enterprises, the capitalists have retained unlimited power. In nationalized factories—formerly the property of "bureaucratic capital"—power is to be invested in a *control committee,* with the manager of the factory acting as president, and consisting of representatives of the former owners, repre-

sentatives of the supervisory personnel and representatives of the workers. But the workers have only *consultative* rights, the director retaining the final say in all decisions (emphasis in the original).[13]

After the occupation of the cities, workers began to raise demands and even attempted to strike against the private employers. The new regime responded by declaring compulsory arbitration of all labor disputes. In many cases workers were forced into accepting wage cuts and into working longer hours; in some cases they had to accept piecework wages. While the government decreed a number of work rules in favor of the workers, its policy was to prevent the workers from taking any independent action.

State trading companies were set up to control trade in foodstuffs, textiles, and other consumer items. Trading cooperatives, already instituted in Manchuria, were expanded into central China. By setting up a "parity index" for commodities and by instituting other controls, the government was able to stem the rampant inflation. After centralizing taxes, imposing surtaxes on luxury items, and levying a "victory loan," it was able to gain financial solvency, so that by April 1950 inflation was brought under control.

Government administrations in the cities were taken over intact and were utilized during the initial reorganization period; their personnel were simply supplemented with trusted cadres. Sections of the old police forces and civil servants thus continued playing the same roles as they did in the Nationalist government.

The peasant reform movement that had been the motive power of the northern drive was not extended into the south after the 1949 victory. In the north—in the old liberated areas—power had already shifted to the newly rich peasants and landowners, some of whom had become party members. In the newly "liberated" areas, the rich peasants and landlords were included as principal components of the local coalition governments. Land reform was not extended to these areas with the takeover, and in February 1950 directives were issued that no redistribution would take place before the harvest in the autumn.

Thus the line of the new government was to complete the bourgeois revolution but not to carry it further. For the first time in China's history, the country was unified politically and economically. While the CCP was the ruling party, the bourgeoisie, petty bourgeoisie, and upper peasantry still had a considerable role in the state apparatus and the economy. Barring a revival of the peasant movement for land reform and a broad-scale working-class movement, the possibility of regroupment of the two old classes remained a potential threat, and the economic future of the country remained to be decided.

Mao presented the perspectives of the CCP in his address to the Seventh Party Congress in June 1950, when he set a three-year timetable to (1) complete the agrarian reform while maintaining a friendly approach to the rich peasants; (2) adjust industry and commerce, especially to improve relations between state and private enterprise; and (3) reduce government expenses, mainly by reducing the size of the People's Liberation Army. The aim here was for gradual reform of society in line with the Stalinist theory of "two stages."

This gradualist approach produced many contradictory problems. While the bulk of industry was state owned, the regime had to aid in the development of private industry. Even though the regime claimed to give leadership to the working class, it imposed many restrictions on working conditions and the ability of the workers to act to improve their wages or conditions. It promised land reform in the future while it favored the rich peasants and held back on promoting the revolution in the countryside. It consolidated the grip of the new bureaucracy instead of promoting mass action to further the revolution. Large sections of the government apparatus were still being administered by the same Kuomintang civil servants.

The new Chinese leaders took a militant nationalist stance in relation to imperialism from the time they came to power. Suspicion and resentment were directed especially toward the United States government for its support to Chiang Kai-shek. This was heightened with the U. S. support of the Chiang regime on Taiwan, and by the fact that U. S. warships patrolled the waters between Taiwan and the mainland. The Mao leadership accused them of plotting to support an invasion by Chiang. All their suspicions rose to a crescendo of anti-imperialism with the outbreak of the war in Korea in June 1950. U. S. intervention was now a direct threat to the Mao regime and it became necessary to consolidate its base. The regime made a left turn in both its internal and foreign policy. This turn was accelerated as Gen. MacArthur's forces threatened the borders of China.

On November 25, China entered the war and found itself faced with immediate retaliation from the United States—in the form of a blockade and the freezing of all China's assets in the United States—and with pressure from the United Nations which endorsed the U. S. actions. Chiang, lying in wait in Formosa, began to make new threats of invasion.

On December 28, 1950, the Government Administrative Council issued a decree taking control of American property and freezing American bank deposits. From that point on, all foreign enterprises were successively taken over.

The opening of the Korean War also posed an internal threat. It gave encouragement to all those who had been opposed to the regime but had lain low. Now oppositions began to manifest themselves, both in the cities and in the countryside. In reaction, the government shifted to the left. It fostered mass mobilizations under the banner of a "Resist America, Aid Korea Campaign" followed by a "Campaign Against Counterrevolutionaries," thus opening up new mass movements in the country.

It was anticipated that the new agrarian law, passed on June 3, 1950, would be carried out gradually, moving from section to section. Central points were set up into which cadre elements were sent to organize committees of agrarian reform. These committees would examine the distribution of land, rents, taxes, usury practices and so forth, after which they would recommend a change to a more equitable distribution and taxation. After completing their work in one area, they would move on to another. Very often in the early period these committees were staffed by intellectuals, rich peasants, and even agents of the landlords. The results were not very promising for general land reform.

During the winter of 1950–51, a shift took place under the impact of the Korean conflict. Peasant committees were reorganized into more representative bodies, with peasants playing a more prominent role. Trials were set up at which the old exploiters would be subject to "speak bitterness" meetings and would be tried and punished on the spot. Punishments ranged from repayment of excessive overcharges, fines for usury, forced labor without pay, to sentences at forced labor camps or even execution for blood crimes. Very rarely were the peasant verdicts reversed.

The next stage saw the distribution of the land and collection of fines from the landlords. After a six-month period, a "verification" made final determination on whether the redistribution had been fairly made, and the government issued certificates of land ownership to the peasants. This revival of land reform swept through all the liberated areas; on the initiative of the peasants, it often went far beyond what the government had intended.

The turn to the left did not mean that the Mao regime became more amenable to the establishment of workers democracy based on workers and peasants councils. Having long since taken shape as a bureaucratic layer interested in the protection of its power and privileges, the leadership sought to assure its dominance in the midst of stormy class struggles through repressions directed both at the right and the left. The Maoist brand of totalitarian rule was established.

A campaign of ideological remolding, directed at the intellectuals, had opened in September 1950. Its aim was to rid the intellectuals of "feudal and bourgeois ideology," "poisonous thoughts," and "ideological decadence." With the opening of hostilities the campaign sharpened and reached all layers of the intelligentsia as well as political opponents. Over the next three years all vestiges of independent thinking were eliminated. Artists, writers, and professors were forced to recant and to go through severe "self-criticism" and ideological remolding. Huge numbers of books on Chinese literature, politics, social studies, and art were burned. Many arrests, as well as suicides, took place. All known Trotskyists were jailed without charges or trial. At the same time a vigorous campaign against Taoist and Christian churches forced many leading figures to recant their religion or leave the country.

Mass trials and executions became common in 1951. The Common Program stated, "Feudal landlords, bureaucratic capitalists and reactionary elements in general . . . shall be compelled to reform themselves through labor so as to become new men."[14] Those convicted were conscripted into such projects as military defenses, railroad building, canals and flood-control projects, and many other types of construction. The numbers of such conscripts is estimated to have run as high as 10 million in 1952.[15] In addition, all those who were suspect were placed under surveillance and deprived of political and other rights, so that all political differences were repressed.

The San Fan (three anti) movement began in November 1951 and was directed at eliminating "corruption, waste and bureaucratism." Mao termed it a "newly opened front." It was directed against the cadres and sections of the state and party bureaucracy, and was, in reality, a form of purge. Huge "struggle" meetings against offenders were held throughout China in the winter of 1951–52. It is estimated that about 4.5 percent of state officials were purged during this period. The San Fan movement thus became another instrument for tightening control over the party and state bureaucracy, as well as for eliminating suspected opponents of the regime.

The Wu Fan (five anti) movement began early in 1952 and was directed primarily at the bourgeoisie. Its objective was to expose the following criminal acts: bribery, tax evasion, fraud, theft, theft of state assets, and leakage of state economic secrets. In China's nine largest cities, over 45, 000 businesses were investigated. Offenders were fined, forced to pay their back taxes, lost many of their managerial powers, and faced imprisonment or forced labor. Many were forced out of business or compelled to accept joint ownership with state management. Many capitalists who had previously hoped for extended coexistence with the new regime now saw the handwriting on the wall.

Thus the turn which began toward the end of 1950, became clearly manifested in 1951 and 1952. The CCP-dominated government eliminated the last vestiges of imperialist influence, seriously embarked on land reform, began eliminating the remaining landlords and bourgeoisie, and purged many of the civil-service holdovers from the Chiang regime.

Despite the limitations of the CCP program and Mao's efforts to involve procapitalist forces in the regime, the victory of the CCP and the People's Liberation Army had set off a deepgoing change in China's political structure.

In the view adopted by the Fourth International, the regime that Mao led at this time was a workers and peasants government which, being compelled to make important inroads into capitalist political and economic power, was moving in the direction of establishing a workers state.[16]

Nationalizations of industry and commerce proceeded at a steady pace:

> By October 1952 nationalization extended to about 80 percent of the heavy industry, and 40 percent of the light industry; the government operated all of the railways and about 60 percent of the steamships plying the home waters; it controlled 90 percent of all loans and deposits through the People's Bank; finally state trading companies were responsible for about 90 percent of imports and exports, for about half of the wholesale trade and for about 30 percent of the retail trade.[17]

In November 1952, a state planning commission was set up to prepare the first five-year plan, modeled on the Soviet plans. It was formally announced on December 24 by Chou En-lai. Its stated objectives were "the establishment of the foundations of the industrialization of the state and the modernization of the national defenses." The major concentration was to be on heavy industry, machines, fuel, and electric power. The process of integration of industry brought more and more factories into the nationalized sector while Soviet economic and technical aid brought China's economy more into line with the Soviet economy.

With the major land reform completed in 1952, the emphasis shifted toward the building of collectives. This was preceded by the setting up of marketing and supply cooperatives, which were integrated into the state monopolies under control of the Ministries of Commerce, Food, and Finance. The cooperatives would buy the crops; fix the prices; sell the salt, fertilizer, and industrial products to the peasants; and lend them money when they ran short. Mutual aid teams helped carry out the larger scale projects for reaping the harvest, for flood and water control, road building, etc. All this set the stage for the actual institution of cooperatives by the end of 1952.

In February 1953 Chou En-lai reported that "there is a great expansion in the agricultural mutual-aid and cooperative movement. In the old liberated areas, organized peasant households now average more than 65 per cent of the whole, and in the newly liberated areas they generally account for some 25 per cent."[18] The exact nature of these "organized households" was not made clear, since the developing forced march toward collectives met considerable resistance from the peasants.

The rapid shift to collectivization produced a decline in productivity instead of the hoped for growth. Bureaucratically organized campaigns drove cadres into forcing peasants into the cooperatives. Inefficient planning in preparing the crops, failure to properly distribute materials to the districts, and other bureaucratic foul-ups produced considerable disorganization. Cadre-driven emulation campaigns, high quotas, and speed-up increased the resistance. All this, combined with a series of natural calamities, resulted in severe shortages of food over the winter of 1952–53, which sent an influx of peasants to the cities.

By spring the CCP decided on a retrenchment, while a period of self-criticism and reexamination took place. Typically, the lower cadres bore the brunt of the criticism for improperly carrying out their directives, for their "impatience," and for not recognizing the "objective conditions" of the peasantry. However, by the end of 1953 the CCP leadership decided to move ahead on its collectivization program and opened a new campaign.

A similar situation arose in industry. After setting high quotas for the Five Year Plan, the CCP tried to drive the workers to meet them and failed. Production fell short of the goals and even, in some cases, dropped back. The workers were faced with exhortations to speed up, and to work longer hours. The accident rate soared and absenteeism became a serious problem. Workers were blamed for lack of discipline, lack of consciousness, and wastefulness; officials were blamed for adventurism and irresponsibility; cadres were blamed for "erroneous concepts." In reality, the low level of education of the workers, their inexperience, the bureaucratism and poor planning of the officials and the cadres, all contributed to the failure to meet quotas, to the extensive waste and shoddy products. The administration was forced to cut back on its targets after only three of the thirteen major quotas were fulfilled.

All this resulted in retrenchment and general reexamination by the CCP. It decided to be more cautious in projecting goals and to be more careful in planning.

> Thus it was that by mid-1954 major decisions had been made in China with regard to such measures as food rationing, a government food monopoly, increase in food exports, and stepped up collectivization. All of these measures indicated Peking's recognition that industrialization could not be accomplished by political control and propaganda alone and that the major part of the cost would have to be borne by China's agriculture.[19]

It was at this stage that socialist objectives were publicly posed as the goals of the regime. In the spring of 1953 local elections and a national census were held for the purpose of convening a National People's Congress to ratify a new constitution. As part of the preparation for this gathering a new "general line" was formulated for "the new period of transition to socialism." "Socialism" in this context meant a workers state.

In 1953, joint state-private ownership was introduced into most industry that had not already been taken over, and a five-year plan was adopted. Thus all of industry and transportation and much of trade was, for practical purposes, in the hands of the state. The power of the capitalists had been broken in the economic and political spheres.

As these changes became widely known, revolutionary socialists around the world concluded that a point of qualitative change had been reached, making it correct to now designate the People's Republic of China as a deformed workers state. The International Secretariat, one of the two factions into which the world Trotskyist movement was then divided, took note of this in a resolution adopted in June 1954, "Rise and Decline of Stalinism." After a thorough discussion, the Socialist Workers Party reached the same conclusion in its 1955 resolution, "The Third Chinese Revolution and Its Aftermath."[20]

In his report on the draft constitution on September 15, 1954, Liu Shao-ch'i indicated his recognition of the qualitative change. He described the new constitution as being of a "socialist" type, not of a "bourgeois" type:

> Life in the past five years has fully proved that the only correct path for our country to take is to pass from our present society, with its complex economic structure, to a society with a unified socialist economic structure—that means transition from the present new democratic society to a socialist society.
>
> It is impossible for the two conflicting relationships of production, socialist and capitalist, to develop side by side in a country without interfering with each other.

He then outlined the types of ownership that existed:

> State ownership, that is ownership by the whole people; cooperative ownership, that is collective ownership by the working masses; and capitalist ownership. The task of the State is to strengthen and extend the first two categories.

He added a footnote: "In the transition period, the national bourgeoisie has a definite status in political life."

He concluded on the theme that the new line of "marching toward socialism" will replace the previous central tasks of "fighting against imperialism, feudalism and bureaucratic capitalism."[21] The new constitution closely followed that of the Soviet Union, many sections duplicating the latter almost word for word.

The line enunciated by Liu Shao-ch'i was put into action in 1954 and 1955. Planned food buying and supply gave the government virtual monopoly of foodstuffs, and furnished its major source of international exchange. The Soviet Union contracted for the completion of 141 heavy industrial enterprises (either new or modernized) to expand the industrial base. Nationalization and collectivization were stepped up.

In 1956 a massive nationalization campaign virtually wiped out the remains of the private sector in industry and trade. Private industry, whose share of production was 39 percent in 1952, approached zero in 1956. Similar changes took place in wholesale trade and, to a lesser extent, in retail trade.

The 1955 Socialist Workers Party resolution summed up the process:

> The objective dynamics, the inner logic of the struggle against imperialist intervention forced the bureaucracy to break with capitalism, nationalize the decisive means of production, impose a monopoly of foreign trade, institute planning, and in this way clear the road for the introduction of production relations and institutions that constitute the foundation of a workers state, which China is today, even though a Stalinist caricature thereof.[22]

During this period China's ties with the Soviet Union steadily tightened. Over 70 percent of its foreign trade was with the Soviet Union and the Eastern European countries. Soviet technicians were sent into China in quantity to supervise installation of Russian equipment and to train Chinese technicians. A study of the Stalinist version of the history of the Soviet Union became mandatory among the cadres. Joint military and diplomatic actions made these ties more binding. Whatever frictions existed that led to the later break were, during this period, completely subordinated to the cooperation between the two countries.

China also broadened its contacts with the colonial world. In June 1954 Chou En-lai and Jawaharlal Nehru met and set up what they term the "Five Principles of Coexistence." These included mutual respect for each other's territorial integrity and sovereignty, non-agression, noninterference in each other's internal affairs, equality and mutual benefit, and peaceful coexistence.[23] In 1955 China was a leading participant in the Bandung Conference. While it stressed an anti-imperialist line more than the Soviet Union, its policies were completely in the orbit of Stalinism.

Stalinist methods were also copied in the conduct of internal affairs. Policy and discipline descended from the top echelons down the bureaucratic ladder. Democratic forms and control by the rank and file in the party were limited to discussion on how best to carry out the policy of the leadership. All oppositions, either from the right or the left, were repressed. Stalinist police methods are an integral part of the Mao regime. As the Socialist Workers Party resolution states, "The collision of Stalinism with each of the sequences of the permanent revolution on Chinese soil has deformed the revolution and obscured its proletarian nature." "China is a deformed workers state because of the Stalinist deformation of the Third Chinese Revolution."[24]

The solution proposed by the SWP resolution to the presence of a bureaucratic caste in the Chinese workers state was an antibureaucratic political revolution. While preserving the gains already made, the change would set China on the road of workers democracy and internationalism.

The Mao regime which took power in 1949 unified the country for the first time. Large sections of industry belonging to the Chiang Kai-shek clique were nationalized. Under pressure of the Korean war the regime turned left. As a workers and peasants government, it carried out extensive land reform, began large scale collectivizations of agriculture and extended its nationalizations. In 1953 it inaugurated its first five-year plan and began posing socialist objectives. A workers state was thus established, a fact codified in 1955 with the adoption of a "socialist" constitution.

CHAPTER FOUR
CUBA

All the early accounts of the Cuban revolution acclaimed the twelve men in the Sierra Maestra. While the twelve did play a central role, it must be stressed that they could not have won without a broad underground support movement throughout Cuba as well as among the anti-Batista Cubans in Miami, New York, Mexico City, and Puerto Rico. Castro won the support not only of the peasantry, but also of the urban workers and numerous members of the middle class and professional groups. He even had adherents in the army, church, and government. The basic objectives of the movement were adherence to the democratic provisions of the constitution and national liberation.

At least six other groups committed to the overthrow of Batista engaged in negotiations with Castro for united action. What was common to them all was adherence to bourgeois democracy. The July 26 Movement began to adopt a more radical orientation after its experiences with the Sierra Maestra peasants, but it was still willing to make programmatic compromises with the other groupings.

For example, on July 12, 1957, Castro issued his *Manifesto From the Sierra*, written with the agreement of Raúl Chibás, son of the founder of the bourgeois Ortodoxo Party, and Felipe Pazos, former president of the Banco Nacional. Significant points included in the manifesto were united action of "all political revolutionary and social sectors that combat the dictatorship"; "truly free, democratic, impartial elections . . . presided over by a provisional, neutral, government"; "divorce the army from politics"; "establishment of the foundations for an agrarian reform that tends to the distribution of barren lands and to convert into proprietors all the lessee-planters, partners and squatters . . . with prior indemnification to the former owners"; "acceleration of the process of industrialization."[1] There was nothing in this document that suggested steps in a socialist direction.

In response to a question by Lee Lockwood on his views at that time Castro stated, ". . . I considered myself a revolutionary. If you asked me, did I consider myself a Marxist-Leninist, I would say no."[2]

What distinguished Castro and the guerrillas from the other groups was that they were determined to stake everything in the struggle and carry it through to the end. They saw the role of imperialism and its lackey Batista, and were determined to end its influence in Cuba. But they never tried to theoretically examine what was necessary to achieve it. In fact they avoided programmatic debates that would have separated the different groupings.

When Lockwood asked, "If you had announced that you were a Marxist and openly espoused a socialist program while you were still a guerrilla leader in the Sierra Maestra, do you think you still would have been able to come to power?" Castro responded, "Possibly not. It would not have been intelligent to bring about such an open confrontation."[3]

The Stalinist Popular Socialist Party (PSP) played no role in the early stages of the anti-Batista struggle. The PSP had worked out a modus vivendi with Batista and played a conservative role. It used its influence in the unions, which it led, as a bargaining point with Batista. It called Castro a "putschist" and was critical of his movement. Only after some important victories were won by the July 26 Movement and its growing support among the masses became apparent did the PSP reconsider. In the middle of 1958, after negotiations for joint action were held, PSP leader Carlos Rafael Rodríguez joined the guerrillas in the Sierra. Throughout the next period and after the victory, the PSP played a completely subordinate role to the July 26 Movement.

The main support and base of the guerrillas was the peasantry. In a country like Cuba, where the sugar crop provided the main economic base, this was crucial to victory. Che Guevara put it most concisely: "At that same time, as the peasants began to participate in the armed struggle for freedom of rights and social justice, we put forth a correct slogan—land reform. This slogan mobilized the oppressed Cuban masses to come forward and fight to seize the land. From this time on the first great social plan was determined, and it later became the banner and primary spearhead of our movement."[4]

The July 26 leaders did not discount the importance of the working class in the cities and especially of the agricultural workers on the huge plantations. But as a result of the frictions between the different organizations, Castro insisted on the leadership of the "mountains over the plains" and the subordination of all activity to the armed struggle of the guerrillas. Activity in the city took the form of providing supplies and funds, intelligence and propaganda, strikes and limited actions of sabotage and other harassing actions. A general strike called for April 9, 1958, failed as a result of inadequate preparations and poor contact. As the military victories grew, support broadened in massive waves, and activities in the cities broadened in like manner. Batista's flight on the last day of 1958 left the July 26 Movement in leadership of a country exploding with revolutionary fervor. A new general strike prepared the way for Castro's triumphal entry into the city.

The first government was a coalition based on the 1940 constitution that had been disregarded by Batista. On Castro's initiative Dr. Manuel Urrútia, a jurist who did not belong to any party, was named president. Dr. José Miro Cardona, President of the Bar Association, was named prime minister, while officials from other organizations, as well as some from the July 26 Movement, rounded out the cabinet. It was a body without any unified program or policy. Castro at first refused any government post; then, under pressure, he took the post of commander of the armed forces.

Economist Edward Boorstein writes:

> When Batista fled, the Rebel Army took over not only the forts and camps of the large cities, but the military posts and police stations everywhere. It was not only the mainstay of revolutionary power, but the embodiment of revolutionary authority in the towns and countryside. The Rebel Army constituted a revolutionary administrative apparatus spread throughout Cuba.[5]

In a very short time differences in outlook between the revolutionists around Castro and the government became apparent.

Castro gave a clear picture of the situation:

> In the hands of the ruling class at this moment were: all the financial resources, all the economic resources, the entire press, all of radio; that is to say, all the big radio and television stations, the big printing presses.... They held all these resources in their hands, the economic resources ... they were, to put it simply, still the owners of the country.... Of course, we were the ones to put him [Urrútia] there; in other words, it was simply due to the Rebel Army ... that a president of the republic was proclaimed....[6]
>
> I recall that in those early days the responsibility for making revolutionary laws was left in their hands.... Throughout that whole period, we waited to see what would happen.... The first weeks went by and they had not passed a single revolutionary law. We had to put up with this because some of those gentlemen had a certain following among the people....[7]

Summary executions of the most prominent military butchers and members of the hated secret police took place before July 26 firing squads. When the imperialists raised the howl of "Castro the butcher," public trials were held before mass juries of the population. Evidence against each prisoner was carefully documented and, when guilty verdicts were reached, executions were promptly carried out. A total of some 600 were executed, a small number compared to the tens of thousands jailed, tortured, and murdered by Batista's henchmen. This did not stop the continued charges in the imperialist press about "Castro brutality."

The contradiction arising from governmental inaction and Castro's propounding radical objectives had to be resolved. Cardona offered to resign on January 17, only to have his offer rejected. By February 12 Castro recognized that a shift was necessary, and Cardona's resignation was accepted along with those of some other members of the cabinet. On February 16, Castro became prime minister, with the mandate to put his objectives into effect.

Castro's twenty-point program included an agrarian reform, (the specific provisions of which had not yet been worked out), "protective tariffs, industrialization to provide 200,000 jobs the first year and an additional 200,000 the second year, a low-cost housing program, salary increases, reductions in salaries of ministers, a solution to the casino [organized crime and gambling] problem, reduction of rents, reduction of public service rates, a new metropolitan area for the capital, creation of the merchant marine, and support of the Gran Colombian Fleet, promotion of a national motion-picture industry, creation of an undersecretary of state for Latin-American affairs, end of all war crime trials in fifteen days, a campaign to consumer national products, a campaign against traffic accidents, a campaign to buy bonds of the Savings and Housing Institute and a World Fair for Cuba."[8] This was still a program of reform rather than social revolution.

The key agrarian reform law was passed on May 17, 1959. It was a serious attempt to solve the problem instead of enacting some token measures, as the middle and upper classes hoped. The law limited large landowners to retaining up to 1,000 acres of their estates (3,000 acres in special cases). Sharecropping was prohibited while a minimum holding for a peasant was set at 66 acres. All land expropriated was to be handed over to cooperatives or distributed in parcels to peasants, free of charges. Agricultural lands henceforth could only be inherited or sold directly to the state, thus preventing any further build-up of large estates.

Compensation for expropriated land was to take the form of twenty-year government bonds at 4.5 percent interest. Enforcement was put in the hands of the National Institute of Agrarian Reform (INRA) which was given the task of promoting cooperatives wherever possible. The country was divided up into twenty eight Agrarian Development Zones for purposes of administration and development, and INRA was given its own juridical powers to enforce its rulings, thus becoming an "autonomous entity." To give INRA further power, Castro took the position of president. INRA was staffed by army leaders, who followed their wartime practices of assuming whatever authority they felt was necessary to achieve their objectives. Property of Batista's henchmen was expropriated outright.

The turn to cooperatives in large-scale agricultural operations was taken at Castro's insistence. It was based on recognition that the predominance of large plantations and estates had already trained a major section of the peasantry to cooperative labor, making the transition to cooperative and state farms comparatively easy. In addition, efficient production required large-scale machine cultivation not possible on individually own plots.

Together with the cooperatives, "tiendas del pueblo" (people's stores) were set up, as were cooperative management of refineries, factories, distribution systems, farm equipment, etc. The effect of the law was indeed far-reaching. To quote Che Guevara, it proceeded "like a tractor or a tank."

Edward Boorstein comments:

> But the takeover of the land proceeded peacefully. The landholders protested against the land reform, both individually and through their associations. They tried to salvage as much as possible of their property and to sabotage the Revolution. They began to turn their physical assets into money to transfer out of the country. They increased their rate of cattle slaughter; cut down their expenditures on fertilizers; bought almost no new equipment; and neglected plowing and planting. But they did not physically resist takeover of the land; the power of the Revolution was too great.[9]

At the same time, a broad program of building new housing and schools made the revolution very concrete to the peasants.

Resistance to these steps had political repercussions. Urrútia, who had become more and more opposed to Castro's actions, vainly tried to hold them back. He was forced to resign by mass demonstrations in July 1959, and was replaced by Osvaldo Dorticós, a staunch supporter of Castro. As the regime swung to the left, it was also resisted by other liberal members of the government, producing a virtual split. Basing himself on the enthusiastic support of the masses, Castro eliminated them one by one.

Relations with the United States deteriorated as the government moved left. "The attitude of the revolutionary government already had been too bold," Castro said in his speech to the United Nations, September 26, 1960. "It had clashed with the interests of the international telephone trust; it had clashed with the interests of the international mining trusts; it had clashed with the interests of the United Fruit Company; and it had, in clashing with these interests, clashed with the most powerful interests of the United States...."[10]

The United States threatened to drop the sugar quota and restrict the export of vital manufactured goods, as well as arms. It began to demand cash payment for exports. Planes began to appear over Cuban skies, bombing and burning cane fields and mills. Defectors began to concentrate in Miami to provide a pool of vengeful opponents of the new regime.

A key problem was to establish economic independence from the United States. To that end Guevara was sent on a tour in June 1959, to Egypt, India, Japan, and the workers states to increase trade. As the United States tightened its restrictions on Cuba, the new government found it increasingly difficult to maintain the dollar reserves needed for foreign trade. Felipe Pazos, president of the National Bank, was an orthodox bourgeois economist who found himself unable to cope with the rapidly changing situation. Che Guevara was put into the office in November 1959, and he immediately put restrictions on the import of nonessential goods, tightening up on all the financial drains on the economy. In addition, he geared the banking system to conform with the movement toward land reform and nationalizations.

It is also a fact that Che's promotion in November 1959 to president of the National Bank marked a decisive turning point in the direction of the Revolution. From that moment on, socialist measures began to rain down with the force of a tropical storm. Later in 1960 Che took charge of the industrial department of INRA, which led, in fact, to his assuming the leadership of the nationalized sector of the economy.[11]

The series of changes in the policies and personnel of the government signified the end of the coalition government. Imperialism was being challenged, land reform was sweeping the country, the banking system was being revamped, and the masses were mobilizing on an ever-broadening basis.

With the fall of Urrútia and the dismissal of Pazos, the Cuban government had declared its independence of the bourgeoisie. It was now a workers and peasants government.

It was a government still in transition. Nationalizations had only begun, and government intervention into other economic spheres was still in its initial stages. There was no clearcut program, perspective, or general plan; the leadership operated empirically, trying to solve problems as they arose. There were no large organized political parties outside the July 26 Movement and the Stalinized PSP that could present and argue for different policies.

The government functioned by decree and appointment to posts rather than by elections and decisions of representative bodies, such as soviets. What gave the government its revolutionary vitality and dynamism was its responsiveness to the needs of the masses and its reliance on mass mobilizations—operating in effect by popular consensus. The masses became deeply loyal to this leadership and every critical stage saw huge turnouts in support of their actions.

Foreign trade underwent a shift in 1960. Anastas Mikoyan, a Soviet leader, arrived on February 4 at the head of a trade mission and worked out an agreement for credits and trade with the Soviet Union. This was a major blow at the U.S.-sponsored policy of restricting trade with Cuba. The agreement with the Soviet Union was then supplemented with trade agreements with China and the Eastern European countries.

In April, 300,000 tons of petroleum were purchased from the Soviet Union. When the three refineries in Cuba—Standard Oil, Texaco, and Shell—were asked to process the oil, they refused. This was the final step in a campaign by these companies to starve Cuba by letting the reserves be depleted. The companies prepared for a showdown and the government retaliated by "intervening" the refineries and operating them under government control. This put into motion a chain of actions and reactions.

On July 7, President Eisenhower ended the sugar quota, cutting off imports to the United States, and Castro countered by nationalizing some American properties. Castro's response: "They will take away our quota pound by pound and we will take away their sugar mills one by one," had broad public support. On August 6, Castro announced the nationalization of all major American-owned sugar mills and land, refineries and other oil properties, as well as the electric power and telephone companies. In September, the Cuban branches of American banks were nationalized. Castro warned, "We will nationalize them down to the nails in their shoes," and everyone knew he meant it.

During this period, additional sugar treaties were made with the Soviet Union and China, thus swinging the major portion of Cuban trade toward the workers states. The United States retaliated by putting an embargo on all exports to Cuba except food and medicines. Even in these items trade declined rapidly. In response, the Cuban government immediately ordered replacement items from the East European countries.

Nationalization of foreign-owned industry had immediate repercussions on Cuban-owned factories, which had been industrially integrated with them. Owners found it difficult to operate private plants for any extended period where the main factories were government-operated. As a result, nationalizations carried over progressively to Cuban-owned enterprises, to the railroads, port facilities, and those enterprises engaged in foreign trade. Thus, in a short period Cuba made the transition from an economy that had been predominantly privately owned to an essentially nationalized one.

By the end of 1960, roughly 80 percent of Cuban industry was nationalized. This included all the strategic industries that produced more than 90 percent of Cuba's exports. The state ran the banking system, railroads, ports, airlines, department stores, hotels, bars, cafeterias, and movie houses. Joseph Hansen observed that "Cuba is one of the most thoroughly nationalized countries in the world."[12]

State farms now comprised about 30 percent of the total farmland, while the rest of agriculture was dominated by collective farms. Foreign trade now was fully under state control.

During the summer of 1960, the first steps were taken to set up a general economic plan. It was organized under the direction of the Junta Central de Planificatión [Juceplan] in February 1961. With the transformation of property relations, Juceplan moved rapidly to set up a planned economy for Cuba, basing itself on the experiences of the Soviet Union, China and Eastern Europe.

The counterrevolutionary invasion at the Bay of Pigs in 1961 led the leaders to begin openly proclaiming the socialist character of the revolution. Within weeks the Cuban masses were proudly celebrating their socialist victory at giant May Day rallies.

These views were in sharp contrast to the leaders' statements of 1959. "Our revolution is neither capitalist nor Communist!" "Our revolution is not red, but olive green, the color of the rebel army," Castro had proclaimed on May 21, 1959.[13] These disclaimers, which continued throughout 1959, were dropped in 1960.

In an interview with Herbert Matthews in 1963, Castro gave more details about this transition:

> It was a gradual process, a dynamic process in which the pressure of events forced me to accept Marxism as the answer to what I was seeking . . .
> So, as events developed, I gradually moved into a Marxist-Leninist position. I cannot tell you just when; the process was so gradual and so natural. [However, answering a question, he agreed that it could well have been mid-1960.][14]

In an interview with Lisa Howard, Che Guevara gave his answer to the question whether he had foreseen the radical outcome of the revolution while he was in the Sierra Maestra. "Intuitively, I felt it," Che said. "Of course, the course and the very violent development of the revolution couldn't be foreseen. Nor was the Marxist-Leninist formulation of the revolution foreseeable. That was the result of a very long process...."[15]

What was distinctive about the Cuban transition as compared with that of Yugoslavia or China was its speed and the clear-cut nature of its stages. In an interview in August 1960, Armando Hart, Minister of Education, put his finger on one vital cause:

> United States policy is forcing us to make our revolution much faster than we wanted to. It is a stupid policy, because the reaction is always the contrary of what the United States wants. Communism was no problem here. If it is now you [the U.S.] created it by forcing us into policies for which we had no other choice.[16]

Thus in a series of rapidly moving but clearly defined phases the Cuban revolution moved from a struggle in which democratic demands were paramount to the establishment of a workers state. The process started with the agrarian reform instituted in May 1959 that began to transform the main economic base of the country, pitting the Castro leadership against the imperialist and bourgeois interests.

The ending of the coalition with the national bourgeoisie in mid-1959 opened the stage of a workers and peasants government. Under this government extensive nationalizations took place from July to October of 1960. The institution of a monopoly of foreign trade, the beginning of planning, and the clearly expressed socialist orientation of the leaders indicated that the nationalizations had transformed Cuba. A workers state now existed.

Politically the revolution did not keep up with the economic developments. The July 26 Movement was not a Leninist party. Proletarian democratic forms, such as the Russian soviets, were not established. Control rested with Castro and the thin layer of leaders who set policies and saw to their execution. While the leaders had the enthusiastic support of the workers and peasants, the masses could not express their views through organized institutions for rank and file discussion and decision.

CHAPTER FIVE
ALGERIA

The Algerian revolution rose on the wave of colonial upsurge that swept Asia and Africa after World War II. The first action of the Algerian National Liberation Front (Front de Libération Nationale—FLN) was a guerrilla attack on November 1, 1954, against the French in the Aures mountains of Eastern Algeria. This took place just six months after the French defeat at Dienbienphu—a defeat that accelerated the disintegration of the French colonial empire.

Independence from France had been advocated by various Algerian movements from 1925, when Messali Hadj, with the backing of the French Communist Party, formed the first organization committed to this goal among the Algerian émigrés in France. After the fall of France in 1940, many more Algerians began to advocate independence, including some of the bourgeois intellectuals and the Ulema (religious intellectual Moslems). Following the war, support for independence grew rapidly.

The economic causes for the movement were clear. In 1954 the *colons* (French settlers, also known as *pieds noirs*) comprised only 11 percent of the population, yet they held 42 percent of the industrial jobs. Ninety percent of industrial and commercial activity was in European hands. The best agricultural areas were controlled for the most part by the *colons*, who owned large, modern estates.

In contrast, the Algerian people were exploited and repressed. Undernourishment was the norm for the majority of the native population. Ninety percent of the population was illiterate and only one Moslem child in ten went to school. All "dangerous" Algerian leaders were either jailed or subjected to house arrest while Algerian representation in the legislative bodies and in the civil service was of a strictly second-class character.

In 1955 the independence struggle began to grow rapidly. The FLN tried to incorporate all the pro-independence groupings from the backward, religious tribal leaderships to the labor and radical movements, as well as the liberal bourgeoisie. The one exception was the Algerian Communist Party, which, because of its tie to the French Communist Party, had supported French repression of the liberation movement. The FLN also won some support from Morocco, Tunisia and Egypt. After a period of factional struggle with Messali Hadj, the FLN also gained the allegiance of Algerian workers in France who were a significant factor in the movement.

Against this liberation struggle, France threw the full weight of its modern army, supplied with the latest weapons from NATO. In the seven-and-a-half-year war more than 400,000 French troops—including almost two-thirds of the air force and half the navy—engaged in the war. The French also used the most refined counterinsurgency methods. In addition to planes, tanks, and naval blockade, they used electrified barriers to seal off the borders of Tunisia and Morocco, operated dragnets to isolate the rebels, and wiped out more than 8,000 villages in a scorched-earth program. They employed the most sophisticated and diabolic methods of terror, espionage, and torture in the attempt to smash the liberation movement.

Casualties were extremely high. Two and a half million persons were displaced as a result of the war, and more than a million deaths were directly attributed to it. More than 300,000 orphaned children flooded the cities, while 300,000 other Algerians were driven into Tunisia and Morocco, where they became an additional base of the liberation struggle.

In spite of all these measures, the French controlled much of the country only by day. The rebels controlled half of it by night.

The war produced severe economic and political strains on an already weakened France. Its repercussions caused the downfall of the "socialist" government of Guy Mollet and the Fourth Republic, bringing the Bonapartist government of De Gaulle into power in 1958. De Gaulle saw that a military solution to the Algerian problem was not possible and he sought ways to resolve the conflict through a political settlement. He offered the Algerians ostensible political equality in a so-called "peace of the brave" that still maintained French hegemony over Algeria. The response of the FLN was to set up a provisional government in exile in September 1958, and step up the fight for independence.

Massive demonstrations in the cities of Algeria in 1960 demanding independence convinced De Gaulle that real concessions, including formal independence, would be necessary.

The *pieds noirs*, who comprised the main base for French rule in Algeria, violently opposed any concessions. When De Gaulle offered the Algerians three choices—integration with France, independence, or independence in cooperation with France (in each case requiring assurances that French capital would continue to play the dominant role)—the *pieds noirs* called for the overthrow of De Gaulle. At one point they almost succeeded in an attempt to assassinate him. In spite of this opposition, a referendum was held in France in January 1961 in which the majority of the French voted to grant Algeria the principle of self-determination, thus opening the way for negotiations with the FLN.

The FLN was far from a united organization. Among the original groups that began the liberation action, there was little agreement on policy beyond the goal of independence. There were differences between the radicals in the cities, the bourgeois nationalists under Ferhat Abbas, the leaders of the feudalistic tribes, and the religious Arab intellectuals who wanted to maintain the old Islamic traditions. Even the most advanced leaders, who considered themeselves socialist, spoke of socialism only in a broad general sense. They had no ties with any international tendency in the world radical movement. Ahmed Ben Bella's ideas, for example, were summed up in his statements, "I am a believer in socialism, short of Marxism," and "No socialism without Arabization."[1]

Another factor was the the Algerian Liberation Army (ALN) military arm of the FLN. Since the FLN leadership was based outside Algeria while the ALN operated within its borders, there was often friction between the two. The ALN had its own political organization that often conflicted with the decisions of the FLN. The ALN had set up six military districts (wilayas), each having its own commander and its own popular base, often the local tribes or clans, and operating with only limited control from the center. Since there was no uniform program and no real central authority, cliquism and factionalism were built into the liberation movement.

Complicating the situation within the liberation movement was the army of Algerian exiles—driven from their country by the genocidal assaults of the French army—formed under the command of Houari Boumedienne in Tunisia. Tightly organized and disciplined, and indoctrinated in a spirit of militant nationalism, this army was being prepared for the day when it could participate fully in the final liberation of Algeria from the French. In the meantime, it was largely restricted to harassing French forces in the border regions.

The decision of the *pieds noirs* to engage in a bloody struggle to prevent independence created a highly explosive situation. Organized into the Organisation l'Armée Secrete (Secret Army Organization—OAS), they engaged in every form of terror, sabotage, and disruption. Their murderous attacks took hundreds of Algerian lives and intensified the bitterness that French rule had engendered.

After a period of negotiations, the Evian agreements were signed between the De Gaulle government and the FLN in March 1962. They provided for a cease-fire, an Algerian referendum on independence, a provisional government to rule during the interim, provision for payment for French property taken over by the Algerians and for French citizens to become Algerian citizens, and an agreement that Algeria would remain in the franc zone. The FLN was recognized as the legitimate, legal authority in Algeria. They agreed on cooperation in exploiting Saharan oil and other minerals, with the French providing technical, economic, and cultural aid. The French were to reduce their armed forces stationed in Algeria by

90 percent within a year, but were allowed to maintain a naval base for fifteen years. French atomic testing in the Sahara was allowed for. With this agreement De Gaulle hoped to maintain French economic control over the country.

On April 8, a referendum in France approved the Evian agreements, and preparations were made for the referendum in Algeria. At this point the OAS undertook its last desperate campaign of sabotage and murder. Its members blew up schools, libraries and hospitals, and laid waste to whatever public buildings, factories and oil installations they could attack. They made a special point to burn or destroy public records. Finally, they organized a boycott of the referendum. After the treaty was approved by an almost unanimous vote, the *pieds noirs* began their exodus to France.

In May 1962, all the principal FLN leaders met to work out their policies for the soon-to-be-independent nation. The leaders now included Ben Bella and three others of the "historic nine" or "historic chiefs" (the leaders who headed the original revolt in 1954) who had been captured and jailed by the French in 1956. Acting members of the provisional government, the army and wilaya commanders, as well as other prominent figures, participated in the meeting. Their objective was to work out a political program and set up a political body to assume leadership. They ratified what is known as the Tripoli Program.

The Tripoli Program represented the views of the most radical section of the leadership, many of whom looked to Ahmed Ben Bella. It was a revolutionary document. Arslan Humbaraci, a newsman who was close to the leadership, claims it was written by Mohammed Harbi, who was aided in the task by Lotfallah Soliman, identified by Humbaraci as an Egyptian Trotskyist, and Michel Raptis, a leader at that time of the Fourth International. While the document was accepted by the conference, it quickly became clear that many of the participants did not agree with it and had no intention of carrying out its more radical provisions.

The Tripoli Program pointed to the mass participation in the struggle as opening a new phase in Algerian history. It stated that "the Evian agreement constitutes a neocolonialist platform which France is ready to use to propagate its new form of domination"; that Algeria suffered from a feudal history and mentality that had to be overthrown; that the feudal gentry had developed into an alien administrative caste; that the new layers of the proletariat and subproletariat, the youth and the women must carry the revolution forward to a socialist perspective; that this vanguard would be able to develop a political ideology, reflecting the aspirations of the masses into a popular revolution; that a new Algerian Arab scientific culture would develop out of the revolution; that the Algerian economy, shattered by the war, would not be developed by foreign capital but would have to develop from the participation of the masses and leadership in a program of planning and nationalization that would eliminate the power of the monopolies; that only a broad agrarian reform, based on mechanization and collectivization, could raise the economic level of the mass of peasantry; that the program must aim toward nationalization of basic industry, transport, banks, and foreign trade, with workers participation in management. All of this was to be achieved in collaboration with the other colonial movements against imperialism.[2]

In addition, the document carried a not-too-veiled attack on the right wing of the FLN, which it claimed still maintained "naive conceptions of authority, the absence of rigorous criteria, and political ignorance [which] favor the development of a feudal mentality."

The conflicts, inherent in the diverse composition of the FLN, came to a head at the conference. After considerable maneuvering, the left-wing forces around Ben Bella won a majority of the proposed political bureau, upon which the supporters of the provisional government walked out. In spite of deepgoing differences, the Tripoli Program was adopted unanimously by the remaining delegates.

Within a short time two rival blocs were formed. On the one side was the group led by Ben Bella, supported by the exile army under Boumedienne and by three of the six wilaya commanders. This grouping advocated going beyond the restrictions of the Evian accords, in line with the socialist principles put forward in the Tripoli program. Although this group had its own internal divisions, it was generally supported by the left wing of the nationalist movement.

The second group under Ben Khedda, the president of the provisional government, was supported by the bourgeois nationalist Ferhat Abbas and by three other wilaya commanders. They advocated close ties with France and the establishment of a regime similar to the pro-French regime of Bourguiba in Tunisia. This wing, however, could not avoid paying lip service to socialist goals as well.

Both sides prepared to campaign for a majority of the assembly, while complicated negotiations were carried on among all the contending forces.

The scope of mass support for the Ben Bella-Boumedienne wing, which often pointed to the Cuban revolution as its model, compelled the Ben Khedda-led Provisional Government to yield power to Ben Bella's Political Bureau.

Then, to the dismay of the country, hostilities broke out between Ben Bella's forces and the guerrilla forces of Algiers, who feared being pushed aside by the new regime. Mass demonstrations forced an end to the fighting.

On September 25, five days after national elections were held, the assembly met with Ferhat Abbas presiding. Ben Bella's cabinet was approved.

The problem of rebuilding the devastated country was enormous.

The exodus of 800,000 *pieds noirs* left vast gaps. In Ben Bella's words:

> Everyone remembers the situation we inherited. Everything was deserted—communication centers, prefectures, and even the administration so vital to the country. When I entered the prefecture of Oran, I personally found just seven employees instead of the 500 who had previously worked there. The departure of the French attained a proportion of 80 percent, even 90 to 98 percent in some technical services such as the highway department. And to that you must add the loss of all statistical records burned or stolen...[3]

To replace the French, Ben Bella found it necessary to rely on the thin layer of educated and skilled middle class Algerians, who moved into government posts and managerial jobs. In a country that was 90 percent illiterate, there was no alternative.

The streets of the cities were crowded with peasants driven off the land during the war, as well as thousands of homeless children. Unemployment in the working class rose to as high as 75 percent. Speculators in abandoned farms, villas, and small factories as well as empty apartments (all termed *biens vacants*) blossomed into a new layer of entrepreneurs aiming to get rich quick. In many cases government officials and wilaya leaders participated in the practice.

On August 24, a decree on the *biens vacants* put all unoccupied premises under the protection of the state if the former owner did not return in thirty days. In follow-up decrees on October 23, management of abandoned farms was to be by committees elected by the farm workers, with the manager appointed by the committee. A month later, a similar decree put vacant factories under control of management committees. Thus "self-management" became part of government policy. While self-management of the farms obtained a good foothold, self-management of the factories never developed adequately. There was no organization to push it, no credits for buying materials, and little provision for marketing the products.

As the only legal political organization, the FLN found itself torn by conflicting currents representing the different economic and political interests. These were expressed in shifting alliances between groups and individuals, often switching from sharp opposition to collaboration, without any clarification of the differences that had separated them. The formation of factions with clearly delineated positions never developed, so that issues were not clarified but often appeared to be personal squabbles.

Although linked by personal views and factional allegiances to the left-wing forces in the FLN, Ben Bella played the role of a conciliator, making concessions first to one group and then to another in hope of maintaining the unity of the FLN and his own leading position within it. Ben Bella admired and often claimed to emulate Fidel Castro, but he lacked the latter's firmness of will and readiness to break with bourgeois forces, including sections of his own July 26 Movement. Where Castro would have called on the masses for support, Ben Bella often chose to maneuver among cliques in the FLN.

There was broad and enthusiastic support among the masses for the radical measures Ben Bella proposed. Probably the most important organization to support his leadership was the Union Générale des Travailleurs Algériens (General Union of Algerian Workers—UGTA), the national labor federation based on 200,000 urban workers. The UGTA was the most advanced social layer in the country. Originally founded in 1956 it became fully active in Algeria only after 1962. It had a strong prosocialist orientation. Many of the workers had been in, or associated with, the Communist Party at one time or another, while a number of its leading members had spent time in the Soviet Union or Eastern Europe.

While supporting Ben Bella's forces, the federation tried to increase its own weight. This brought it into conflict with Ben Bella, who took the view that the Tripoli Program placed the UGTA under the control of the FLN. Negotiations ended in a temporary compromise that was blown up at the UGTA Congress in January 1963. Ben Bella insisted that the UGTA must be an arm of the FLN and could not fight for higher wages and better conditions as an autonomous organization; that it had the duty, instead, to play an active part in running the economy, making the promotion of production, and not wages and working conditions, its primary aim. During the sessions, FLN Secretary-General Mohammed Khider brought in several hundred goons who took over the sessions, and forced the pro-autonomy leaders to resign. This action took the heart out of the militant wing in the unions, so that it ceased for a time to play a significant role.

The Algerian Communist Party (PCA) was banned shortly after independence in the name of the need for a single-party state. It continued to operate semi-legally in fact. Its newspaper, *Alger Républicain*, was not suppressed and was widely read. Leading PCA members were in the editorship of *Révolution Africaine*, the prominent monthly FLN journal, until they were replaced by the left FLN group under Mohammed Harbi. The Communists, often giving critical support to Ben Bella, operated mainly within the UGTA and the Union Nationale des Etudiants Algériens (National Union of Algerian Students—UNEA).

The UNEA was a continuation of the organization that had existed throughout the war; it maintained a limited independence, even though Ben Bella made several efforts to put it under the control of the FLN. Its leadership was faction-ridden from the start, and it never achieved the effectiveness that the left wing of the FLN expected of it.

Women played an important role in the liberation war, serving as couriers, in intelligence work, in underground combat, and in many other aspects of the struggle. They saw independence as a great step in the direction of equality. They demanded elimination of the veil, the symbol of inferiority and backwardness. The Tripoli Program declared as its goal the achievement of the equality of the sexes. However, after independence, women found it even more difficult than before to get jobs, to obtain posts in the ministries and the self-managed factories and farms. They found themselves up against the wall of male prejudice at every turn. Their organization, the Union Nationale des Femmes Algeriennes (National Union of Algerian Women—UNFA), could not get the cooperation of the government as promised, and was not able to build an active organization that could play a role in the life of the country.

On March 29, 1963, Ben Bella—reacting to a French nuclear test in the Sahara—announced the famous March decrees, which gave permanent status to the nationalized sector of the economy. The divisions in his regime were exposed in the preparations for issuing the decrees. They were not raised inside the FLN for discussion and vote. Nor were they submitted to the National Assembly for its approval. Instead, they were announced by Ben Bella on his own initiative and with the endorsement of only part of his cabinet. They produced a split in the leadership, with Khider and Ferhat Abbas going into opposition.

The decrees established (1) what were considered vacated property (*biens vacants*) and in effect nationalized; (2) the rules for the organization and self-management of industry, agriculture, and commerce through the election of management committees by general assemblies of the workers, but with the directors appointed by the government; (3) the allocation of the profits from the enterprises—one part to the workers and the other part to the state for purchase of new equipment, new investments, and an employment fund.[4]

Another decree set up the Office Nationale de la Réforme Agraire (National Office of Agrarian Reform—ONRA) to carry out the agrarian reform and to set up state farms. An additional decree set up the state-controlled marketing system.

Ben Bella then went on a national tour to build support for these far-reaching economic steps. His popularity was at a high point, since the decrees set objectives that coincided with the needs and hopes of the most militant sections of the population. However, it was clear that the period ahead would be the most critical since the effectiveness of these steps remained to be tested.

During the next three months, extended nationalizations of European-owned enterprises took place. Many enterprises that had been bought by Algerians at the time of independence were also taken over. By June more than 1.5 million hectares of land were under self-management (one hectare equals 2.47 acres). UGTA and FLN trucks carried thousands of workers to the rural areas every week to aid the peasants and to renew their confidence. National campaigns for reconstruction and restoration were undertaken. Mass meetings became a standard means of building enthusiasm as well as providing basic education in the aims of the administration.

On February 17, 1964, the United Secretariat of the Fourth International issued a statement summarizing the views of the world Trotskyist movement on the character of the Algerian government. It held that the period initiated by the March decrees marked a point of qualitative change:

> For some time the course of the new regime in Algeria has shown that it is a 'Workers and Peasants Government' of the kind considered by the Communist International in its early days as likely to appear, and referred to in the Transitional program of the Fourth International, as a possible forerunner of a workers state.

The statement indicated the significant dates in the process of the new regime's formation as follows:

> An essentially bourgeois state apparatus was bequeathed to Algeria. A crisis in the leadership of the FLN came to a head July 1, 1962, ending after a few days in the establishment of a de facto coalition government in which Ferhat Abbas and Ben Bella represented the two opposing wings of neocolonialism and popular revolution. The struggle between these two tendencies within the coalition ended in the reinforcement of the Ben Bella wing, promulgation of the decrees of March 1963 and the ouster successively of Khider, Ferhat Abbas and other bourgeois leaders although some rightist elements still remain in the government. These changes marked the end of the coalition and the establishment of a Workers and Peasants government.[5]

In 1969, a resolution adopted by the International Executive Committee of the Fourth International reaffirmed this judgment:

> The rising curve in the revolution reached its highest point with the March 1963 decrees and continued up to the expropriation measures in October of the same year. Observing this process, the United Secretariat of the Fourth International took note of the fact that a workers and peasants government had been established in Algeria.[6]

The establishment of this kind of government signified an unavoidable showdown in the near future with the bourgeois forces backed by imperialism. If Ben Bella failed to move decisively to replace the capitalist system with a new social order, resting on the mobilizations of the workers and peasants to accomplish this, the bourgeois forces would attempt to overthrow the new regime.

Land ownership by the French was eliminated by October 1963, affecting about 4 million hectares. While they encompassed only a small portion of the farmlands, they contributed about 60 percent of the national agricultural product. They were now operated by 200,000 permanent agricultural workers, about one-tenth the total in the country. Some 40 million hectares of less productive land remained in the hands of the more backward fellahs and were cultivated by the old, primitive methods.

The worker-managed industrial plants, in contrast, comprised but a small section of industry which was largely owned by wealthy colon or Algerian families, or by local affiliates of international concerns. The approximately 450 enterprises of the nationalized sector were swamped by the 2,500 in the private sector. Lack of trained workers, inexperienced managers, the refusal of banks to grant loans—these and other difficulties put the nationalized sector at a disadvantage. A complete dearth of trained accountants made it almost impossible for anyone in the self-managed sector to get a clear picture of production, sales, inventories, or profits.

At the heart of the problem was the lack of political or economic preparation by the government for instituting workers' management as well as the regime's inability to rise to the political needs of the situation. It was hampered by the lack of education of the workers, their limited skills, as well as the terrible shortage of active leaders. There was also poor leadership from the FLN—in fact few plants had party cells that functioned. In some cases, state officials, opposed to self-management, took advantage of this situation to scrap the management committees and give the directors full power.

The government made a heroic effort to train personnel to fill the gaps, but the effort fell far short of the requirements. By the end of 1963, the government had appointed only 25 directors to enterprises when 450 enterprises needed them. By the end of 1964, almost one-third of the state farms had no accountants, and the majority of those that did had accountants who had completed a six-month crash course. As a result, rapid deterioration of self-management set in. Workers' assemblies bogged down or disbanded. Scandals, misuse of materials, breakdown of equipment, diversion of material for private use, and even outright embezzlement began to seriously undermine the functioning of many plants and farms. Salary payments were often delayed, in some cases as much as three months. The movement toward self-management thus ran into the hard realities of social and political backwardness, as well as the obstruction and sabotage of the opponents of socialist aims.

As the government's radical turn developed in the context of a deepening economic crisis, leaders of the liberation movement began to oppose Ben Bella. While the differences were often obscure, some of the opponents (such as Ait Ahmed and Mohammed Khider) provided channels for the bourgeois and landlord opposition.

In September 1962, at the time of the elections to the National Assembly, Mohammed Boudiaf, one of the "historic nine," went into opposition and set up a clandestine organization called the Party of Socialist Revolution. Its program, however, differed little from that of Ben Bella. Later Boudiaf moved to the right, denouncing Ben Bella's measures as too precipitate. In February 1963, Major Si Larbi, a wilaya commander of the Constantine region, openly challenged Ben Bella. Ben Bella was able to unseat him and force his retirement from the army.

In June, the arrest of Boudiaf for conspiracy was followed by a violent clash between Ben Bella and Ait Ahmed, another of the "historic nine." Ait Ahmed then withdrew from the assembly and retired to his native Kabylia (an ethnic area east of Algiers) to organize another opposition. After that Belkacem Krim, another "historic nine" leader, broke with Ben Bella and went into opposition.

At the same time, a struggle was taking place between Ben Bella and Mohammed Khider, secretary-general of the FLN. Riding the popularity gained from the March decrees, Ben Bella was able to displace Khider and assume the post of secretary-general himself. Khider then left the country to become another oppositionist.

Yet another dispute arose over the constitution. The assembly was supposed to have drawn it up, but because of its inability to do this, (about one-third of the members could not even read or write) the political bureau of the FLN stepped in to produce the draft. After completion, the draft was submitted to the FLN for approval; then, after an elaborate ceremony, it was submitted to the National Assembly, meeting in mid-1963. Ferhat Abbas, president of the assembly, resigned in protest over the procedure, but later admitted that his real reason was opposition to the radical course of the government.

The constitution states that "Algeria is a Democratic and Popular Republic" that "is an integral part of the Arab Maghreb, of the Arab World and of Africa." It decrees that "Islam is the religion of the state." A major amount of authority is vested in the president who is elected by direct popular vote. The president not only initiates legislation, carries out foreign policy, and appoints ministers, but is also head of the armed forces and appoints all civil and military personnel to leading positions. The constitution provides for only one party, the FLN, which "carries out the objectives of the democratic and popular revolution, and constructs socialism." It defines the policy of the nation and controls the actions of the National Assembly and government. Thus the president and the FLN play the dominant role in the government, going to the assembly only for approval of their actions.[7]

The draft aroused sharp criticism from the procapitalist sections of the assembly. Objections centered on the broad powers of the president and the lack of adequate checks upon him. Yet when it came to a vote, the constitution was adopted overwhelmingly. It was then presented to the country in a referendum and approved almost unanimously. With the direct vote of the population, Ben Bella became the elected president on September 15, 1963.

Two opposition groups took shape, forming separate, armed, clandestine groups, neither one having broad support. Both groups called for "socialism" and the overthrow of Ben Bella, but they never clearly delineated their differences with each other—or with Ben Bella for that matter. Boumedienne opened a military campaign against the two groups, but, in the midst of this conflict, a border dispute developed with Morocco that led to a three-week armed conflict.

When Ben Bella, on October 15, called upon the nation to mobilize for war, the opposition leaders immediately came out in full support of the government and volunteered to fight in defense of the country's border. This momentary unity added to the confusion in the population about the nature of the differences between the contending forces.

In July 1963 various oppositional groups had unified into a Committee for the Defense of the Revolution with offices in Switzerland. By the fall of 1964, two-thirds of the 50,000-strong army were fighting guerrillas in the countryside. Rebellions by wilaya commanders Si Larbi and Mouhan el-Hadj ended with their arrest and imprisonment. The leader of another rebel force, Colonel Chaabani, was arrested and shot after a secret trial.

After his election as president, Ben Bella prepared for the convention of the FLN. In the two years of independence the party had grown to 153,000, with another 619,000 "adherents" or candidates for membership. Its organization was very loose. Membership was based as much on alliances and friendships as on political qualifications. Control over the party units was weak, especially in the smaller towns and villages. "The typical small-town official was a young man dressed in a French-cut suit and Italian pointed shoes, hiding behind dark glasses and posing as an intellectual," wrote David and Marian Ottaway.[8] Ben Bella never felt strong enough to rid the FLN of all the doubtful members, and it remained a field for aspiring bureaucrats aiming at personal status and privilege.

One of the aims of the congress held April 16–21, 1964, was to reestablish party unity and restate the objectives of the FLN. The document produced, called the Algiers Charter, was written by Mohammed Harbi and Abdel Aziz Zerdani, left-wing leaders of the FLN. The charter restated the social and economic program of the government and its socialist perspective. It denied any conflict between socialism and Islam. It declared that self-management expressed the will of the working class to emerge on the political-economic scene and establish itself as the leading force. It was the stated objective of the FLN to extend self-management to the entire economy. At the same time the charter pointed to the danger that the single party and the powerful presidency could lead to a dictatorship as a result of the irreconcilable internal contradictions. The document also pointed to the danger of a growing "bureaucratic bourgeoisie" (a reference to administrators who used their positions to accumulate wealth, through bribery and control of nationalized industry), as well as the continued existence of sections of the former colonial administrations.[9]

Conflicts again emerged at the congress. This time the army faction headed by Boumedienne disagreed with the orientation toward "Marxist" rather than Nasser-style socialism. Boumedienne's group made it clear that it wanted no part of any campaign against FLN bureaucrats. The faction claimed this would further divide the country or even lead to civil war. While they opposed many sections of the charter, Boumedienne's supporters had no one ready to propose an alternative, so the vote for the charter was unanimous. The deep divisions thus remained—to explode at the next crisis. In the new central committee and political bureau, Ben Bella's forces held a slight edge.

While the Algerian government took a strong anti-imperialist line, its leaders did not want to break economic ties with France, fearing that such a course could result in hundreds of thousands of Algerians facing starvation. French policy was designed to maintain maximum economic interest in Algeria. In exchange for financial and technical aid, and for special trade agreements, the Algerian government was willing to make concessions.

Algeria remained the fourth most important market for French products, while 75 percent of Algerian exports went to France. About 23,000 French teachers and technicians were sent to Algeria during the first three years, while France extended loans that amounted to $800 million. About half a million Algerians emigrated to France to serve as a low-paid source of labor. In a country where fulltime employment hardly reached one million, with about 1.2 million unemployed, the overseas labor outlet was an extremely significant factor that served to maintain the tie between the two countries. Algerians were able to send home $60 million a year, which comprised a significant portion of the national income.

France was vitally concerned with protecting its $2 billion oil investments in the Sahara. It had the controlling interest in the exploration, extraction and refining processes that were ostensibly worked on a cooperative basis. It paid royalties for the products at a lower rate than those paid to other countries. It was only in 1965 that a new agreement was signed, making Algeria a major partner in the exploitation of its oil, as well as providing training for Algerian personnel to fill key production and management posts.

The French rulers were acutely conscious of the lessons of the U.S. imperialist defeat in Cuba and their own failure to defeat the Algerian revolution by military means. Instead of trying to bring the Ben Bella regime down through economic blockade, military subversion, and hysterical redbaiting, the French preferred a subtle combination of financial pressures, economic aid, and a friendly diplomatic stance that seemed to offer the promise of more concessions and aid. In this way, they encouraged Ben Bella's tendency to temporize and compromise with irreconcilable enemies of the Algerian revolution. At the same time, the French imperialists did what they could to foster opposition to the regime's radical policies, particularly by cultivating ties with developing conservative layers in the army.

Thus, when Ben Bella reacted to a French nuclear test in the Sahara by announcing the sweeping nationalizations of March 1963, the French did not react by breaking off all relations. Instead they quietly increased economic pressure while offering diplomatic concessions in the form of renegotiating aspects of the Evian accords. The new agreement guaranteed some important French interests, while the French went so far as to favorably mention some of Ben Bella's favorite leftist conceptions, such as "peasant socialism."

Jean de Broglie, French secretary of state in charge of Algerian affairs, stated the view of the French government very clearly. "Algeria must not be for France what Cuba is for the United States," he said. "Cooperation, to survive, will have to be adapted with realism to a situation profoundly modified by the injuries done to the patrimony of the French in Algeria. . . . In the present conjuncture, French policy, pragmatic above all, is attempting to defend with vigor the fundamental interests of France without breaking the privileged relations, which for multiple reasons, unite the two states."[10]

In September 1963, Ben Bella, on a visit to the Soviet Union, was granted $100 million in credits for arms and industrial materials. This breakthrough was followed by loans from the East European countries, China, and Cuba. In the next few years, the Soviet Union increased its aid. None of this was adequate, however, to ease the chronic economic crisis in Algeria or lessen its dependence on France.

Ben Bella was the single most popular figure in Algeria, but he failed to use that popularity to decisively break the opposition to socialist measures, and thus reorganize the economy on a new basis. As a result the economic crisis deepened, unemployment continued to plague the country, and the peasants on whose support he had relied became largely passive politically. To revive the revolution would require mobilizing the urban masses on a massive scale, a course Ben Bella did not follow. As a result, his popular support declined.

Self-management stagnated and conflicts in the leadership sharpened. The UGTA grew increasingly restive over the failure of the government to extend nationalizations and expand union control of production. Government officials tried to restrain union activity in the private sector, fearing that harassment might force the owners to close down. Production dropped sharply and employment declined. Strikes took place at an increasing rate, and efforts were begun to organize the unorganized establishments, bringing a new spirit into the unions. When an owner closed a plant down, the union often moved to nationalize it, only to have Ben Bella admonish the union leaders not to "force" nationalization at too fast a pace. Under rank and file pressure, Ben Bella gave unions control of training and promotion of personnel in private companies. Then the labor leaders promoted a new organization of farm workers—the Fédération Nationale des Travailleurs de la Terre (National Federation of Agricultural Labor—FNTT), aimed at the largest bloc of labor in the country. But by doing this, the union came into a direct clash with the heads of the Ministry of Agriculture, who objected to union interference with their management of the nationalized farms. Militant workers were fired for union activity, while the government officials tried to stack the leadership of the new union with their own people and to housebreak it.

The issue came to a head at the December congress of the FNTT. Leaders of both the UGTA and the ONRA (the government office in charge of the nationalized farms) jockeyed for control, and the ONRA officials won out. In his speech to the congress, Ben Bella warned the ONRA people that they too "could make mistakes," but he made no effort to reverse their bureaucratic operations. The congress followed what was becoming a familiar pattern. Delegates were permitted to speak and criticize freely, but when the time came for motions, the ONRA officials, working constantly behind the scenes, carried all their objectives.

Leaders of the UGTA, stung by this defeat, began to put pressure on Ben Bella to back them up. Hoping to recover his standing with them, he agreed to give them more support at the next UGTA congress, scheduled for March 1965, if they would play more of a managerial role in production and not a "Western" role in supporting strikes for higher pay and better working conditions.

At the UGTA congress, Ben Bella continued to play the role of mediator, warning against "extremism" and emphasizing the need to follow a "normal development" of socialism. But this time he was met by vigorous opposition from the ranks. Secretaries' reports were voted down by large margins. Secretary-General Rabah Djermane, a close friend of Ben Bella, was accused of shirking his duties, of apathy, and of inaction; his report was voted down by 201 to 24, with 234 abstentions. Less than half of the outgoing members of the executive committee were reelected, and they were supplemented by more militant representatives of the workers. Also, for the first time, two women were elected to the executive. To the enthusiastic applause of the delegates, a new militant leader, Mouloud Oumeziane, was elected Secretary-General. The congress ended with an emotional speech by Ben Bella, who promised that by the end of the year the socialist sector would dominate the private one.

This alliance of the more militant unions and Ben Bella opened a new phase in the country's politics, pointing to the polarization of the socialist and antisocialist forces. Ben Bella still tried to combine the bureaucratic wing that had supported him with the more militant unionists and other political forces. He made his peace with the Communist Party in October 1964, and it became active in the bloc. On the other hand, under pressure from the religious Islamic section, Mohammed Harbi was dropped as editor of *Révolution Africaine* and was replaced by a representative of "Islamic socialism."

The right wing began to consolidate as the struggle sharpened. Guerrilla actions by the CDR increased, as did right-wing demonstrations in some major cities. The government bureaucracy became increasingly resistant to any radical change, and the religious groupings hardened their stand against any further moves in a socialist direction.

Ben Bella had come into leadership of the government with the support of Houari Boumedienne's exile army, and the regime's tenuous stability had depended on this alliance between the two. While this army included a core of professional military cadres trained by France who had thrown themselves into the national struggle, and also incorporated Algerian elements of the French army who remained after independence, it was essentially a peasant-based army organized around the anti-French struggle. The army was identified at first with the FLN left wing.

However the army was organized on a hierarchical basis. Thus its officers were inclined to look askance at Ben Bella's preoccupation with workers and peasants control. In a country afflicted with poverty, unemployment, homelessness and near-starvation, the army alone was a source of steady jobs and steady pay. For this reason, it tended to become an elite layer with a stake in aid from abroad, social peace, and economic stability. As Algeria stagnated and Ben Bella hesitated to adopt a revolutionary course, the army and its high command moved steadily rightward. Policy differences erupted openly at the 1964 FLN congress; there, the army faction stood in defense of what the FLN charter called the "bureaucratic bourgeoisie."

The friction stemmed from the army's social character as an elite force that was becoming closely linked to the conservative state bureaucracy, to bourgeois elements in Algeria, and to the imperialists. This brought the army into conflict with Ben Bella, who acted as the vacillating head of a political movement that rested on the workers and peasants.

The Algerian workers and peasants government was now divided between a developing procapitalist wing and a confused and hesitant left wing.

After the clashes at the 1964 FLN congress, Ben Bella began to try to undermine Boumedienne by forcing pro-Boumedienne ministers to resign, until the only prominent one left was the foreign minister, Abdelaziz Bouteflika. In May 1965, Ben Bella came into conflict with Bouteflika over the preparations for the forthcoming Afro-Asian Conference to be held in Algiers. When Ben Bella requested his resignation, Bouteflika refused. Shortly after, on June 19, Boumedienne, with the aid of some of Ben Bella's former allies, carried out a military coup that ousted Ben Bella from power. It took place on the eve of the conference, which was never held. Ben Bella has been held prisoner ever since.

The coup was carried out without significant opposition, testifying to Ben Bella's loss of his mass base. Many of his allies and supporters opened talks with Boumedienne to see if they could collaborate with him; there was no leader willing to take a firm stand in opposition. Some actions were taken by left-wing students and Communists, but their demonstrations were quickly broken up. Only in two cities in the western Oran area, where Ben Bella still had some mass support, were there any attempts at mass demonstrations against the coup, but they were dispersed by the army with some casualties.

Even the left wing, led by Mohammed Harbi and Hocine Zahouane, was slow in declaring its opposition. UGTA leaders, after some hesitation, decided to compromise with Boumedienne and took a neutral stance toward the new regime. The country generally accepted the change in leadership but without any enthusiasm. Even though Boumedienne brought several of Ben Bella's former supporters into the government, it was now clear that the army was in control.

About a month after the coup, the various opposition groups, the Communist Party, the JFLN (youth group of the FLN), and the UNEA (the national student organization) formed a unified organization (Organisation de Résistance Populaire—ORP) under the leadership of Harbi and Zahouane. It was forced, however, to become clandestine immediately. In a short time all the major leaders of the different groups were arrested: the ORP and the Communist Party were outlawed. Trotskyist and other radicals were captured, tortured, and jailed. Under the reign of terror, the ORP steadily declined.

The new regime made a steady shift to the right. Some of the richest self-managed farms were handed over to the army, and many nationalized enterprises, beginning with the hotels, were handed back to the former owners. The authority of the FLN was constantly reduced, as was that of organizations of women, students, and youth. Police began to break up strikes. After a dispute, the UGTA paper was suppressed. In June 1966, after some seventy of the most militant leaders were arrested, the UGTA ceased to operate as a viable independent organization.

The new government sought to obscure the sharp turn to the right. In some cases it even carried out projects planned by the Ben Bella regime. A state bank to finance the socialist sectors was announced in May 1966. Eleven foreign mines were nationalized and operated by the state, and the government established a state monopoly over the insurance business. None of the steps included the principle of self-management. There was no attempt to involve the masses; they remained quiescent under the watchful eyes of Boumedienne's police.

Boumedienne also carefully cultivated an international image as a leftist. His financial aid to the Palestinian cause and his anti-Israeli stance helped convince many early critics, such as Fidel Castro, that no fundamental rightward shift had occurred.

In 1969, the International Executive Committee of the Fourth International characterized the effects of the coup as follows:

> The June 19 coup d'état marked the destruction of the workers and peasants government. The molecular changes for the worse, which had been accumulating both in the consciousness of the varied classes and in the government personnel and organization, had ended in a qualitative change. Having seized power with relative ease, owing to the previous deterioration in the situation, Boumedienne and his army had little trouble in putting down the opposition. The new power represented a reactionary resolution of the contradiction that had existed between the capitalist state and the workers and peasants government with its socialist orientation.[11]

The Boumedienne regime differed qualitatively from its predecessor. Ben Bella had taken measures pointing toward establishment of a workers state, relying on the support of the masses to carry them out. The Boumedienne government, in contrast, represented the interests of a developing national bourgeoisie.

The fall of Ben Bella was a sharp reminder that the establishment of a workers and peasants government by no means assures the creation of a workers state. Meeting a seemingly less intransigent response from the imperialists than the workers and peasants governments in China and Cuba had confronted, the Ben Bella regime hesitated, stagnated, and fell.

CHAPTER SIX
CONCLUSIONS

Some general conclusions can be drawn from the course of events in these four countries, permitting us to gain a clearer understanding of the process by which a workers and peasants government can become established, including the steps leading from this to establishment of a workers state.

However, the question remains: How does the reality we have examined square with Trotsky's viewpoint, so clearly stated in the *Transitional Program?* Trotsky, as we noted earlier, wrote:

> The experience of Russia demonstrated, and the experience of Spain and France once again confirms, that even under very favorable conditions the parties of the petty-bourgeois democracy (S.R.'s, Social Democrats, Stalinists, Anarchists) are incapable of creating a government of workers and peasants, that is, a government independent of the bourgeoisie.[1]

While he drew this negative conclusion on the basis of the experience between the two world wars, Trotsky still left open the theoretical possibility that it could occur:

> Is the creation of such a government by the traditional workers' organizations possible? Past experience shows, as has already been stated, that this is to say the least highly improbable. However, one cannot categorically deny in advance the theoretical possibility that, under the influence of completely exceptional circumstances (war, defeat, financial crash, mass revolutionary pressure, etc.), the petty-bourgeois parties, including the Stalinists, may go further than they themselves wish along the road to a break with the bourgeoisie. In any case one thing is not to be doubted: even if this highly improbable variant somewhere at some time becomes a reality and the "workers' and farmers' government" in the above-mentioned sense is established in fact, it would represent merely a short episode on the road to the actual dictatorship of the proletariat.[2]

Trotsky, it is clear, was drawing on "past experience"—that is, the refusal of the Mensheviks and Social Revolutionaries to break with the bourgeoisie in 1917, the short-lived workers and farmers governments in Hungary and Bavaria in 1919, the defeat of the German revolution in 1918 and 1923, the defeat caused by the "bloc of four classes" policy in China and the popular-front betrayals in France and Spain in the 1930s. These experiences did not in any way negate the value of advocating a workers and farmers government as a means of mobilizing, educating, and building mass movements aimed at weakening and eliminating the capitalist regimes.

Trotsky believed that in the process of building the mass mobilization, the revolutionary party would win leadership of the working class. Once having established a workers and farmers government in conjunction with other worker and peasant parties, the revolutionary party would take the lead in bringing about the rapid completion of the process, setting up the dictatorship of the proletariat, and in a brief period making the economic transition to the workers state.

Trotsky believed that "the full dictatorship of the proletariat can only be accomplished by the workers' government composed of Communists."[3]

In fighting for that objective, he indicated some transitional steps:

> Of all the parties and organizations which base themselves on the workers and peasants and speak in their name we demand that they break politically from the bourgeoisie and enter upon the road of struggle for the workers' and farmers' government. On this road we promise them full support against capitalist reaction. At the same time, we indefatigably develop agitation around those transitional demands which in our opinion should form the program of the "workers' and farmers' government."[4]

In the wake of the World War II several workers and farmers governments appeared. In three cases (examined above) they overturned capitalism, going further than Trotsky had thought possible in the absence of a Bolshevik-type leadership. Does this require modification of Trotsky's basic conclusions? Were these transformations historical exceptions? Or do they represent a new historical pattern? To answer these questions correctly we must recall Trotsky's basic postulate.

He held that the second world war would produce revolutionary movements of unprecedented scope, opening the way to workers victories in several *industrially advanced* countries. The key to victory on a world scale, he maintained, would be the building of revolutionary parties—sections of the Fourth International. This would be facilitated by the exposure of Stalinism—an inevitable result of Stalinism's failure to block another world war, its failure to adequately defend the Soviet Union, and its betrayal of workers uprisings.

As always the concrete reality proved to be more complex than the general prognosis. Although a revolutionary wave swept much of Europe and Asia as the war drew to a close, revolutionary parties of sufficient strength did not exist to bring the workers to power. The Stalinists grew stronger for a time because of the popular identification of Stalinism with the victory won by the Soviet Union over German imperialism.

Because of their strength in the workers movement, the Stalinists and Social Democrats were able to prevent the bourgeois order from going down in Europe. In the colonial world, Stalinist and bourgeois nationalist forces blocked the road to proletarian leadership and a socialist outcome.

Although deeply shaken, Western Europe remained firmly in capitalist hands. This created the political conditions for a new capitalist economic boom in the industrially advanced capitalist countries, and for renewal of the imperialist offensive against the Soviet Union and the world revolution in the form of the cold war.

While a worldwide revolutionary upheaval—a distinct possibility in the immediate postwar period—was successfully fended off by the imperialists and Stalinists, the imperialists were unable to win decisive counterrevolutionary victories because of the strength of the anticapitalist forces.

The upshot was a highly unstable world situation that included the following important factors: (1) the decline in power of imperialism internationally, with the United States taking on the central responsibility for world capitalism; (2) the rise of the Soviet Union to the status of second strongest power in the world; (3) the growth of Stalinist parties as a result of the Soviet victory, obscuring Stalinism's counterrevolutionary role and blocking the growth of revolutionary Marxist parties that could challenge them on a mass scale; and (4) the impetus the war gave to a tremendous groundswell of national liberation movements that challenged imperialism and served to weaken it further.

Besides the military defeat suffered by German, Japanese and Italian imperialism, the British, French, and Dutch colonial empires declined, as independence movements that began during the war continued to sap their economic and political strength. Only the United States grew in power and influence, gaining dominance in many areas where other imperialist powers once held sway. The United States became not only the main exploiter in the capitalist world but also its policeman.

Independence movements sprang up across Asia, Africa and Latin America, and continued to develop over the next decades. The four countries studied here were caught up in that process. Yugoslavia and China gained their independence directly from the struggles begun during the war, while Cuba and Algeria derived their inspiration from the wave of colonial movements that developed in the postwar period.

The struggles were directed against the imperialists and their most direct tools, the "compradore bourgeoisie" (native capitalists acting as agents of the imperialists in investment and trade) and the landowning elements bound up with them. Petty-bourgeois leaders of the liberation struggles were more than willing to make agreements with the "progressive" national bourgeoisie to form national liberation fronts. These fronts sought to set up nationalist governments committed to preserving capitalist property relations.

In none of the cases described here did the leadership come to power with a program of building a socialist order. In fact, the policy proposed was invariably one of building "national unity" under a multiclass "democratic" nationalist regime. Leaders like Tito and Mao, who spoke in favor of socialism and thus won considerable popular support, subscribed to Stalin's two-stage theory of revolution—"progressive" capitalism now, socialism later. They used this concept to justify their negotiations for alliances with capitalist and even imperialist forces.

The national liberation movements sought to win the support of the peasants who compose the majority of the population and who are the main base of economic production in colonial countries. Exploited by landlords, banks, usurers and merchants, the peasants bear the greatest weight of oppression. Any movement that offers them hope of economic betterment through national independence and agrarian reform can tap profound reserves of courage and self-sacrifice, as has been powerfully demonstrated in the struggles of the Vietnamese peasants. In each of the four cases studied, the peasants provided the bulk of the soldiers, the main food supplies, and the mass base upon which the armies functioned. This support by the peasants was a decisive element in the victory.

In only one of the four countries—Yugoslavia—did the workers play a central role in the military struggle. In Yugoslavia workers organized the initial forces against the Nazis and provided the shock troops, the "proletarian brigades," that were the most valiant and skilled fighters of the partisan movement. (Even in this case, peasants composed half the party membership at the time of the partisan victory.)

In Cuba, the working-class organizations were not an official part of the July 26 Movement though workers played an important role in supporting the underground, aiding it with supplies and information, and conducting strikes at crucial moments.

Workers also played a key role in Algeria, supporting the FLN in the cities, conducting strikes and other militant actions against the supporters of the French.

In China, working-class participation was systematically discouraged by Mao.

The national bourgeoisie did not play a favorable role in any of the four countries. Those serving most directly as agents of international capital were thoroughly hostile to the mass upsurges, did what they could to beat them down, and finally went into exile. The "progressive" bourgeoisie acted as a drag, attempting to subvert the revolutionary movement through their influence within the coalition governments. Many finally went abroad. Others held on in one way or another, hoping for an eventual turn in their direction.

In all four cases a single party became the undisputed leader of the struggle and was the dominant force after the victory. Using their broad authority the leaders set up coalition regimes, in which they sought to exercise control. They tried to definitively break their main civil-war opponents. This meant expropriating the properties of the compradores (bureaucratic capital in China), landowners, and others who had collaborated with the imperialist forces.

The new governments smashed key parts of the machinery of the old state, especially the army and the political police. The state bureaucracy and police were partially purged and then absorbed, becoming part of the new ruling apparatus and part of the new bureaucracy as well.

The new governments proceeded to institute some of the reforms they had projected, modifying but not qualitatively changing the capitalist economic base of the country.

In *The Permanent Revolution,* Leon Trotsky wrote:

> With regard to countries with a belated bourgeois development, especially the colonial and semicolonial countries, the theory of permanent revolution signifies that the complete and genuine solution of their tasks of achieving

democracy and emancipation is conceivable only through the dictatorship of the proletariat as the leader of the subjugated nation, above all of its peasant masses.[5]

Trotsky's view on this point was completely verified. Those national movements that won independence in countries like India and Indonesia found themselves in a difficult situation. They remained dependent on imperialism for industrial supplies, manufactured goods, equipment and machinery, and even—in some cases—vital raw materials. They were forced to turn to the international banks and imperialist powers for credits and other financial aid. Formal independence did not bring them the benefits of bourgeois democracy; it brought them, rather, colonial status on a different level, in which they achieved neither real national emancipation nor real democracy.

Only where they were able to break from imperialist control and set up workers states were some countries able to make significant economic advances. This happened in Yugoslavia, China, and Cuba. Social revolutions took place in those countries in a distorted form and not in the way projected by Lenin and Trotsky; yet the change in economic system enabled them to make advances that could not be matched in those countries that remained in the capitalist orbit.

The key factor was the winning of independence. In Yugoslavia, the Communist-led partisans were forced to carry on an independent struggle against the German imperialist armies and Mihajlovic without the aid from Moscow that they counted on. They came to power with a greater measure of independence from Moscow than any other Communist party, and with more reservations about Stalin's role. They viewed with suspicion the pressure from Churchill and Stalin to permit the entry of King Peter's representatives into the government, and they stubbornly resisted all attempts at intervention. If they had any doubts as to what their future would be if they acceded, the bloody suppression of the Greek partisans by Britain, with Stalin's acquiescence, must have cleared that up. Their resistance to these pressures drove the Yugoslavs toward independence.

In China, Mao's forces moved toward independence not out of their own initiative but out of Chiang Kai-shek's adamant refusal to collaborate. He brought the war to the Chinese Communist Party, forcing it into a showdown fight in its own defense. Mao's forces took power after the collapse of the Chiang regime, which enabled them to fill the resulting vacuum.

The amount and pace of nationalizations varied in each country and began at a different level. Industrial expropriations ranged from almost none in Cuba at the time of victory to over 70 percent in China. Nationalizations expanded with the pace of confrontations with imperialism. In both Yugoslavia and China, the government was involved from the start in running considerable sections of the economy. In China, land reform, which had been extensive in the north before the victory, was slowed down and limited in the newly liberated areas. In Yugoslavia and Cuba, land reform became extensive soon after the victory. In general, the governments tried at first to set a slow pace, endeavoring to work out collaboration with the remaining capitalists and with the middle and upper layers of the peasantry. What upset their plans was the reaction of the imperialists.

Nationalization of key industries is not uncommon in semicolonial countries under bourgeois rule, and is not by itself an indicator of the class nature of the government. Prevented by their financial weakness from undertaking large-scale projects, the semicolonial capitalists turn to the government to assume the costs. Similarly in the industrially advanced countries, ailing industries are sometimes nationalized and operated by the state. These steps, however, are taken under the direction and control of the capitalist representatives themselves and serve the interests of that class. Invariably they are taken "for the good of the nation" and in some cases even given a socialist coloration, but in every case the nationalizations flow from the needs of the capitalists and are not a threat to them. In the four countries studied, the workers and farmers governments were independent of the bourgeoisie, and the actions were seen as a direct threat to their existence.

The imperialists took either a suspicious or hostile attitude toward the four regimes from the start, and this was hardened by international tensions. The cold war, beginning in 1946, forced the Soviet Union to eliminate capitalist economic forces in the

East European countries, and produced a strong reaction among the Yugoslavs. The Chinese reacted similarly in the Korean War. Both governments tightened their internal regimes, eliminating hostile or potentially hostile elements, and prepared their military forces to resist invasion. With the land reform in Cuba, resulting in a sharply hostile reaction from the American imperialists, a similar development took place there.

Washington's resistance to even limited reforms put the Castro leadership on the spot. Wall Street's attitude, coupled with the pressure of the Cuban masses, drove the regime to consolidate its control over the economy and to move against the Cuban bourgeoisie.

The imperialists tightened the screws on the defiant countries by instituting economic boycotts and blockades and exerting military pressure. This escalation of economic and military aggressiveness was an important factor in shaping the development of the workers and farmers government. Each stage produced a corresponding reaction, facilitated by the fact that as the imperialists cut off trade, Moscow moved in to supply the most needed goods.

In Algeria, the flexible approach of the De Gaulle government served to slow the process of nationalization and to limit land reform to expropriation of the holdings of the pieds noirs. While the impetus of the liberation victory carried the FLN into the stage of establishing a government independent of the bourgeoisie, the continued dependence on France for trade and for financial, material, and technical aid served to undermine its independence, cause divisions in the ranks of the FLN, and provide the impetus for the overthrow of the Ben Bella regime. This contrast between the approach of the De Gaulle government and that of the United States is striking and leads to speculation on what the course of the Yugoslav, Chinese, and Cuban revolutions would have been if the attitude of imperialism toward them had been different.

This review indicates that Trotsky's forecast on the unlikelihood of workers and farmers governments appearing in the post World War II period was not completely borne out. While the formation of these governments flowed from the specific set of circumstances in each of the four countries, they were the result, first of all, of the changed relationships in the postwar world that weakened imperialism and provided greater opportunities for the development of national liberation movements in the absence of mass revolutionary-Marxist parties. In the four countries, the transition was the result of external and internal pressures that drove the leading parties into going much further than they had anticipated. These countries proved, however, to be the exception rather than the rule, for in the majority of cases, after winning independence, the liberated countries fell prey to neocolonialism. By and large, imperialism has maintained its control over the colonial and semicolonial world even though that control is repeatedly challenged.

Once having established workers and farmers governments, the leaders were constantly confronted with new problems that had to be solved. It was not possible to simultaneously move ahead with land reform and pacify the rich peasants. It was not possible to nationalize property and at the same time pacify the remaining capitalists. One side or the other had to give way. The inevitable reaction of the rich peasants and capitalists was to protect their interests by foot-dragging, bribery, diversion of goods, falsification of taxes, and outright sabotage. Any concessions would only have hardened reactionary resistance, for the old ruling class could not settle for less than the restoration of bourgeois governmental power.

Mass pressure for change pushed the process forward. Peasants and workers who had made heavy sacrifices expected promises of social change to be carried out. When the first steps were taken, the masses helped to speed them up. The extension of the land reform into south China by the Mao regime, for example, produced an agrarian revolution that the government could acquiesce in but not stop. The regimes were thus forced to travel farther along the road mapped by the theory of permanent revolution. Radical measures further undermined the possibility of coming to terms with the bourgeoisie. Instead, these forces began to flee the country or carry out subversion that compelled the regime to repress them. This put pressure on the leaders to organize the economy through massive nationalizations and planning in order to prevent the growth of opposition and social instability.

The presence of the Soviet Union as a counterforce to imperialism and an example of a society that had successfully overturned the capitalists was another factor that aided the overturns. Confronted by imperialist economic blockades, the leaderships could turn to the Soviet Union in many cases for aid, trade, loans, military hardware, and technical assistance. While these relations helped the Soviet Union, they were vital to the workers and peasants governments.

In the course of this process of nationalization, land reform, and government control of trade, the leaderships came to realize that they were moving in the direction of establishing workers states, or "socialism," as they termed it. They speeded up completion of the nationalizations and set up collective and state farms as the norm in agriculture. Speaking for the Mao regime, Liu Shao-ch'i said: "It is impossible for two conflicting relationships of production, socialist and capitalist, to develop side by side in a country without interfering with each other."

While it is not possible to point to a specific date in which the workers state came into being in any of the three countries, the moment can be bracketed within fairly narrow limits by the progress of nationalizations, the introduction of planning, government control of finances, establishment of a monopoly of foreign trade, etc. In other words, when the decisive anticapitalist economic changes have been completed, the workers and peasants government has also completed the transition to a workers state.

When workers states were established in China and Yugoslavia, the leaders tried to explain the process by claiming they had followed the path of the Russian Revolution (with national variations). The Yugoslavs propounded the theory of "several roads to socialism" and claimed that socialism had been their objective all along. However, they could not explain why, with the same basic wartime class-collaborationist policies as theirs, the Communist parties in Greece, Italy, and France failed to lead a revolution, even though conditions were ripe for a bid for power.

Similarly, none of the Communist parties have been able to explain why the Communist Party of Indonesia, which followed the same class-collaborationist policies as did Mao, ended so tragically. Nor have the Chinese leaders ever attempted to explain why Mao's policy of forming a bloc of four classes, which Mao claimed was proved valid by the victory in 1949, failed so miserably in 1927, ending with the defeat of the revolution and the decimation of the Chinese Communist Party.

Under Lenin and Trotsky, the Bolsheviks played a conscious proletarian role at every stage of their revolution. They began with a program of socialism and formulated a strategy to achieve it. They applied Marxist methods of analysis to every stage of the struggle, up to and beyond the establishment of the workers state. Above all, they fostered mass democratic organs of the workers and peasants to carry out the revolution thoroughly and completely. They knew that the Russian revolution was only a link in the chain of world revolution. Only the success of the world revolution would make socialism possible; and they worked to advance it.

In none of the four countries were these concepts or practices followed. Under Tito and Mao, Stalinist practices prevailed. Their parties were bureaucratically dominated apparati, lacking democratic-centralist modes of functioning. They applied police methods learned from Stalin to prevent the presentation of alternative views. Only one party was permitted to exist. In the mass organizations, Stalinist methods were used to maintain dictatorial control. The leaders blocked the formation of real soviets. By these methods, Tito and Mao assured the transformation of the party and army bureaucracy into bureaucratic castes of which they were the preeminent representatives.

In Cuba the leaders played a different role. Castro and Guevara were not trained in the Stalinist tradition. They did not, like Tito and Mao, represent a bureaucratic grouping opposed to the free development of the revolution. They had closer ties to the masses, relied more heavily on mass mobilizations, and were more responsive to the needs and wishes of the masses. However, Castro's failure to sponsor organs of mass workers' democracy prepared the ground for the development of bureaucratic deformations, made more severe by the pressures exerted by the Soviet bureaucracy. Castro's attempts to counter this, as indicated in the campaigns against Cuban Stalinist Escalante, did not prevent further adaptation to Stalinist pressure.

Trotsky pointed out that the world situation is chiefly characterized by a historical crisis of the leadership of the proletariat. The truth of this observation was borne out to an extraordinary degree in the decades following the Second World War. World capitalism was seriously weakened in the conflict, opening the possibility for successful revolutions in the advanced countries, especially in France and Italy, that could have changed the course of history. Stalinism is directly responsible for these failures.

Instead of the industrially advanced countries, revolutions took place in the colonial world where middle-class and Stalinist leaderships—under special circumstances—were able to break their countries out of the capitalist orbit, testifying to the increasing weakness of world capitalism. Those victories have given rise to new political trends and to new theories about what constitutes a revolutionary leadership adequate to the task of achieving socialism.

The victories in Yugoslavia and China under the leadership of Communist parties were attributed by some to a new stage in the evolution of Stalinism, or at least to special revolutionary characteristics inherent in these parties. After all, it was argued, they did lead revolutions. In Cuba, however, a non-Stalinist, middle-class, nationalist leadership led a revolution, indicating that these victories were the result of a new objective situation rather than a change in the nature of Stalinism.

The Cuban leaders of the July 26 Movement outflanked the Cuban Communist Party from the left. Lacking the restriction of Stalinist ideology, especially the Menshevik theory of stages, they were able to make the transition to a workers state at a fast rate. However, the Cuban experience gave rise to another theory that gained some prominence—that of guerrilla warfare as the sure path to revolutionary victory. After a series of attempts to duplicate the Cuban experience failed, support for the theory declined, although it is still advocated by some sections of the radical movement.

The role played by the leadership in the four countries under review shows that a revolutionary Leninist party adhering to the program of socialism is by far the best guarantee of winning national revolutions in the colonial and semicolonial countries and of establishing workers states. In the advanced industrial countries, however, *only* a revolutionary party of this type can overthrow capitalism and achieve victory. The concentrated power of the large, cohesive, capitalist class, with centuries of experience in maintaining its rule, can be dislodged only by a skilled, highly trained and disciplined party based on the mass organizations of the industrial proletariat and supported by sections of the middle class and poor peasants.

The capitalists, too, especially those represented by Washington, have drawn some conclusions from what happened in the postwar years. They learned from the morass they sank into in the Korean and Vietnam wars that direct confrontation is a costly business. They learned from the French and from their own experience how to deal more flexibly with a colonial upsurge. They have developed high skill in counter-insurgency operations as a means of combatting guerrilla actions. The CIA has undermined and toppled several regimes that appeared to be challenging American imperialist interests.

Can workers and peasants governments of the type seen in Yugoslavia, China, Cuba, and Algeria appear again? We can agree with Trotsky that it is unlikely; however, experience has shown that it is not quite as unlikely as he thought. It depends on the development of completely exceptional circumstances.

But this is not the main line of historical development. The evidence is mounting that the epicenter of revolution is now turning to the industrially advanced countries. A variant of the pattern of the Russian Revolution seems to be foreshadowed by the current upsurges, particularly in Europe.

Imperialism, even though it was not able to defeat it, was able to prevent the spread of the Russian Revolution beyond the borders of the Soviet Union after World War I. After World War II, imperialism lost control of a much greater area of the world's surface. Each crisis once again poses the question of whether it will be able to maintain its grip on what is left. The next major crisis, be it from war, a financial crash, or revolutionary upsurges, will carry the process still further and bring into question the very existence of imperialism. The completion of the task of transforming the world will be the job of the international revolutionary-Marxist party. This is the aim of the Fourth International.

References

Introduction

1. Joseph Hansen, "The Social Transformations in Eastern Europe, China, and Cuba," in *The Workers and Farmers Government*, (Pathfinder Press, 1974), p. 36 [2015 printing].

Chapter One: Historical Background

1. V. I. Lenin, *State and Revolution*, in *Collected Works*, Volume 25 (Moscow: Progress Publishers, 1964), p. 402.
2. Leon Trotsky, *The Permanent Revolution* and *Results and Prospects* (New York: Pathfinder Press, 1974), p. 278–9.
3. E. H. Carr, *The Bolshevik Revolution, 1917–1923*, vol. 1 (Baltimore: Penguin Books, 1966), pp. 120–121.
4. Ibid., vol. 2, p. 80.
5. Ibid., vol. 2, p. 84.
6. Ibid., vol. 2, pp. 95–96.
7. V. I. Lenin, *Collected Works*, vol. 27 (Moscow: Progress Publishers, 1974), p. 334–5.
8. Ibid., p. 241.
9. Novack, George; Frankel, Dave; and Feldman, Fred, *The First Three Internationals* (New York: Pathfinder Press, 1974), p. 106.
10. Leon Trotsky, *The First Five Years of the Communist International*, vol. II, (Pathfinder Press, 1972), p. 438 [2015 printing].
11. "The Workers Government: Excerpts from the 'Theses on Tactics' and Discussion at the Fourth World Congress of the Comintern," in Joseph Hansen, *The Workers and Farmers Government*, (Pathfinder Press, 1974), p. 53–54 [2015 printing].
12. Ibid., p. 54 [2015 printing].
13. Leon Trotsky, *The Transitional Program for Socialist Revolution* (Pathfinder Press, 1974), p. 175 [2014 printing].

Chapter Two: Yugoslavia

1. Vladimir Dedijer, *Tito* (New York: Simon and Schuster, 1953), p. 189.
2. Stephen Clissod, *Whirlwind* (London: Cresset Press, 1959), p. 111.
3. Ibid., p. 196.
4. Ibid., p. 198.
5. M. Christman, ed., *The Essential Tito* (New York: St. Martin's Press, 1970), p. 25.
6. Boris Kidric, *On the Construction of Socialist Economy in the FPRY: Speech Delivered at the V Congress of the CPY*, (Belgrade: Office of Information of the FPRY, 1948), p. 5.
7. Christman, op. cit., p. 53.
8. Quoted in A. Ross Johnson, *The Transformation of Communist Ideology*, (Cambridge, Mass.: MIT Press, 1972), p. 38.
9. Ibid., p. 39.
10. Kidric, op. cit., p. 31.
11. Dedijer, *Tito*, p. 424–425.
12. Ibid., p. 300.

Chapter Three: China

1. Mao Tse-tung, *On Coalition Government* (Peking: Foreign Languages Press, 1955), p. 1.
2. Jack Belden, *China Shakes the World* (New York: Monthly Review Press, 1970), p. 79.
3. Mao Tse-tung, *Selected Works*, Vol. 3 (London: Lawrence & Wishart, 1954), p. 109, 110.
4. Mao Tse-tung, *On Coalition Government*, op. cit., p. 49.
5. *International Information Bulletin*, April 1952 (New York: Socialist Workers Party), p. 4.
6. Peng Shu-tse and Chen Pi-lan, *The Chinese Revolution: Part I* (Pathfinder Press, 1972).
7. O. Edmund Clubb, *20th Century China* (New York: Columbia University Press, 1964), p. 274.
8. Jack Belden, op. cit., p. 159.
9. *The Common Program and Other Documents* (Peking: Foreign Languages Press, 1950), p. 2.
10. *Fourth International*, New York, Vol. 12, No. 1, Jan.–Feb. 1951, p. 15.
11. Mao Tse-tung, *On Peoples Democratic Dictatorship*, second edition (Peking: Foreign Languages Press, 1950), p. 20.
12. Ibid., p. 22.
13. *Fourth International*, New York, Vol. 10, No. 11, December 1949, p. 330.

14. Richard L. Walker, *China Under Communism: The First Five Years* (New Haven: Yale University Press, 1955), p. 221.

15. Ibid., p. 222.

16. "The Third Chinese Revolution," Resolution adopted by the May 1952 Plenum of the International Executive Committee of the Fourth International, published in *Fourth International*, New York, Vol. 13, No. 4, July–August 1952.

17. Walker, op. cit., p. 106.

18. *Documents of the First Session of the First National People's Congress* (Peking: Foreign Languages Press, 1955).

19. Walker, op. cit., p. 143.

20. "The Rise and Decline of Stalinism," resolution of the "Fourth World Congress" of the International Secretariat of the Fourth International, in *The Development and Disintegration of World Stalinism* (Pathfinder Press, 1970); "The Third Chinese Revolution and Its Aftermath," resolution of the Socialist Workers Party, in *The Chinese Revolution and Its Development*, (Pathfinder Press, 1969).

21. Walker, op. cit., p. 125.

22. *The Chinese Revolution and Its Development* (Pathfinder Press, 1969), p. 6 [2014 printing].

23. Robert V. Daniels, ed., *A Documentary History of Communism*, Volume 2 (New York: Vintage, 1960), p. 346.

24. *The Chinese Revolution and Its Development*, op. cit., p. 6 [2014 printing].

Chapter Four: Cuba

1. Jules Dubois, *Fidel Castro*, (Indianapolis: Bobbs-Merrill Co., 1959), pp. 168–70.

2. Lee Lockwood, *Castro's Cuba, Cuba's Fidel*, (New York: Macmillan Co., 1967), p. 143.

3. Ibid., p. 142.

4. *Che Guevara Speaks*, (Pathfinder Press, 1967, 2000), p. 17 [2013 printing].

5. Edward Boorstein, *The Economic Transformation of Cuba*, (New York: Monthly Review Press, 1968), pp. 37–38.

6. *Fidel Castro Speaks on Marxism-Leninism*, (New York: Fair Play for Cuba Committee, 1961), p. 27.

7. Ibid., p. 32.

8. Dubois, op. cit., p. 375.

9. Boorstein, op. cit., p. 44.

10. Martin Kenner and James Petras, eds., *Fidel Castro Speaks*, (New York: Grove Press, 1969), p. 14.

11. K.S. Karol, *Guerrillas in Power*, (New York: Hill and Wang, 1970), pp. 42–3.

12. Joseph Hansen, Cuban question: Report for the Political Committee (January 14, 1961), in *Dynamics of the Cuban Revolution*, (Pathfinder Press, 1978), p. 114 [2010 printing].

13. Kenner and Petras, op. cit., p. 67.

14. Herbert L. Matthews, *Fidel Castro*, (New York: Simon and Schuster, 1970), p. 186.

15. Ibid., p. 190.

16. Ibid., pp. 191–92.

Chapter Five: Algeria

1. David C. Gordon, *The Passing of French Algeria*, (London: Oxford University Press, 1966), p. 105.

2. *The Tripoli Program*, (Toronto: Workers Vanguard Publishing Association, 1963); Also contained in Thomas L. Blair, *The Land to Those Who Work It*, (New York: Doubleday & Co., 1969), pp. 237–282.

3. David and Marina Ottoway, *Algeria—The Politics of a Socialist Revolution*, (Berkeley: University of California Press, 1970), p. 10.

4. Blair, op. cit., pp. 226–233.

5. "On the Character of the Algerian Government," in *World Outlook* (now *Intercontinental Press*), Paris, Volume 2, No. 8, February 21, 1964, p. 1.

6. "The Algerian Revolution From 1962 to 1969," (1969 Resolution of the Fourth International) in Hansen, Joseph *The Workers and Farmers Government*, (Pathfinder Press, 1974), p. 84 [2015 printing].

7. Joachim Joesten, *The New Algeria*, (Chicago: Follet Publishing Co., 1964), p. 193-201.

8. Ottoway, op. cit., p. 116.

9. Ibid., p. 119–20.

10. "French Imperialism Fears Another Cuba," in *World Outlook* (now *Intercontinental Press*), Paris, Vol. 1, No. 5, October 25, 1963, p. 10.

11. "The Algerian Revolution From 1962 to 1969," op. cit., p. 68 [2015 printing].

Chapter Six: Conclusions

1. Leon Trotsky, *The Transitional Program for Socialist Revolution* (Pathfinder Press, 1974), p. 174 [2014 printing].

2. Ibid., p. 175 [2014 printing].

3. "Excerpts from the 'Theses on Tactics' and Discussion at the Fourth World Congress of the Comintern" in Hansen, Joseph, *The Workers and Farmers Government* (Pathfinder Press, 1974), p. 54 [2015 printing].

4. Leon Trotsky, *The Transitional Program for Socialist Revolution*, op.cit., p. 175 [2014 printing].

5. Leon Trotsky, *The Permanent Revolution and Results and Prospects*, (New York: Pathfinder Press, 1974), p. 276.

BUILDING A PROLETARIAN PARTY

New!
The Fight Against Jew-Hatred and Pogroms in the Imperialist Epoch
Stakes for the International Working Class

V.I. LENIN, LEON TROTSKY
FARRELL DOBBS
JAMES P. CANNON
JACK BARNES
DAVE PRINCE

Jew-hatred and pogroms—like Hamas carried out on October 7, 2023—are now part of the permanent social convulsions and wars of the imperialist epoch. That's why fighting Jew-hatred is of decisive importance to the working class and oppressed nations of the entire world. The authors answer the all-important question: *What is to be done to end it*—for all time. $10. Also in Spanish and French.

The Struggle for a Proletarian Party
JAMES P. CANNON

"The workers of America have power enough to topple the structure of capitalism at home and to lift the whole world with them when they rise," Cannon asserts. On the eve of World War II, a founder of the communist movement in the US and leader of the Communist International in Lenin's time defends the program and party-building norms of Bolshevism. $20. Also in Spanish and Farsi.

In Defense of Marxism
Against the Petty-Bourgeois Opposition in the Socialist Workers Party
LEON TROTSKY

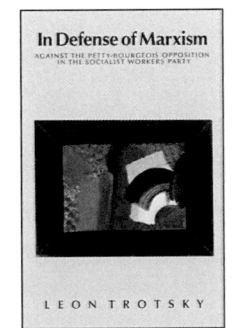

A reply to those in the revolutionary workers movement in the late 1930s buckling to bourgeois patriotism during Washington's buildup to enter World War II. Trotsky explains why only a party fighting to bring workers into its ranks and leadership can steer a communist course. In the process, he defends the materialist and dialectical foundations of Marxism. $17. Also in Spanish, French, Farsi.

The Transitional Program for Socialist Revolution
LEON TROTSKY

The Socialist Workers Party program, drafted by Trotsky in 1938, still guides the SWP and communists the world over. The party "uncompromisingly gives battle to all political groupings tied to the apron strings of the bourgeoisie. Its task—the abolition of capitalism's domination. Its aim—socialism. Its method—the proletarian revolution." $17. Also in Farsi.

Socialism on Trial
Testimony at Minneapolis Sedition Trial
JAMES P. CANNON

The revolutionary program of the working class, presented in response to frame-up charges of "seditious conspiracy" in 1941, on the eve of US entry into World War II. The defendants were leaders of the Minneapolis labor movement and the Socialist Workers Party. $15. Also in Spanish, French, Farsi.

Their Trotsky and Ours
JACK BARNES

To lead the working class in a successful revolution, a mass proletarian party is needed whose cadres, well beforehand, have absorbed a world communist program, are proletarian in life and work, derive deep satisfaction from doing politics, and have forged a leadership with an acute sense of what to do next. This book is about building such a party. $12. Also in Spanish, French, Farsi.

Lenin's Final Fight
Speeches and Writings, 1922–23
V.I. LENIN

$17. Also in Spanish, Farsi, Greek.

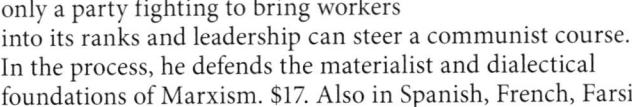

PATHFINDERPRESS.COM

Also from Pathfinder

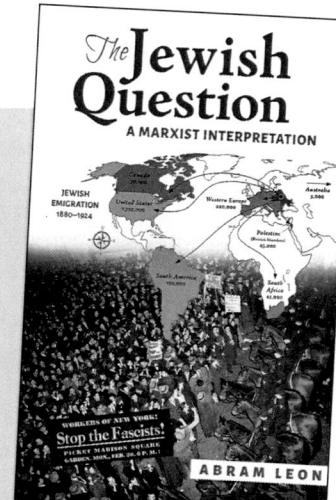

The Jewish Question
A MARXIST INTERPRETATION
Abram Leon

The battle against reactionary forces aiming to exterminate the Jews remains central to world politics, as shown by the genocidal October 2023 pogrom in Israel. Why is Jew-hatred still raising its ugly head? What are its class roots? Why, as Abram Leon explains, is there no solution "independent of the world proletarian revolution"? Revised translation, new introduction, and 40 pages of illustrations and maps. $17. Also in Spanish and French.

The Communist Manifesto
Karl Marx and Frederick Engels

Communism, say the founding leaders of the revolutionary workers movement, is not a set of ideas or preconceived "principles" but workers' line of march to power, springing from a "movement going on under our very eyes." $5. Also in Spanish, French, Farsi, Arabic.

The Teamster Series
Farrell Dobbs

Four books on the strikes, organizing drives, and political campaigns that transformed the Teamsters across the Midwest in the 1930s into a militant industrial union movement. Written by Farrell Dobbs, the general organizer of these Teamster battles and leader of the Socialist Workers Party.

A tool for workers seeking to use union power in every workplace and advance the fight for an independent labor party. $16 each, series $50. Also in Spanish. *Teamster Rebellion* is also available in French, Farsi, Greek.

Malcolm X Talks to Young People

"The young generation of whites, Blacks, browns, whatever else—you're living at a time of revolution," said Malcolm in 1964. "And I for one will join with anyone, I don't care what color you are, as long as you want to change this miserable condition that exists on this earth." Four talks and an interview in the last months of Malcolm's life. $12. Also in Spanish, French, Farsi, Greek.

New International
A MAGAZINE OF MARXIST POLITICS AND THEORY

OPENING GUNS OF WORLD WAR III: WASHINGTON'S ASSAULT ON IRAQ

JACK BARNES

The murderous assault on Iraq in 1990–91 heralded increasingly sharp conflicts among imperialist powers, growing instability of capitalism, and more wars. Also includes:
1945: When US Troops Said No!
by Mary-Alice Waters
Lessons from the Iran-Iraq War
by Samad Sharif
In *New International* no. 7. $14. Also in Spanish, French, Farsi.

CAPITALISM'S LONG HOT WINTER HAS BEGUN

JACK BARNES

Today's global capitalist crisis is but the opening stage of decades of economic, financial, and social convulsions and class battles. Class-conscious workers confront this historic turning point for imperialism with confidence, Jack Barnes writes, drawing satisfaction from being "in their face" as we chart a revolutionary course to take power. In *New International* no. 12. $14. Also in Spanish, French, Farsi, Arabic, Greek.

U.S. IMPERIALISM HAS LOST THE COLD WAR

JACK BARNES

The collapse of regimes across Eastern Europe and the USSR claiming to be communist did not mean workers and farmers there had been crushed. In today's sharpening class conflicts and wars, these toilers are joining working people the world over in the class struggle against capitalist exploitation. In *New International* no. 11. $14. Also in Spanish, French, Farsi, Greek.

The Low Point of Labor Resistance Is Behind Us
THE SOCIALIST WORKERS PARTY LOOKS FORWARD

Jack Barnes
Mary-Alice Waters
Steve Clark

The global order imposed by Washington after its victory in World War II is shattering. A long retreat by the working class and unions has come to an end. The bosses and their government are stepping up attacks on our wages, conditions, and constitutional rights. This book highlights opportunities for building a mass proletarian party able to lead the struggle to end capitalist rule, opening a socialist future for humanity. $10. Also in Spanish and French.

Labor, Nature, and the Evolution of Humanity
THE LONG VIEW OF HISTORY

Frederick Engels, Karl Marx
George Novack, Mary-Alice Waters

Without understanding that social labor, transforming nature, has driven humanity's evolution for millions of years, working people are unable to see beyond the capitalist epoch of class exploitation that warps all human relations, ideas, and values. Only the revolutionary conquest of state power by the working class can open the door to a world free of capitalist exploitation, degradation of nature, subjugation of women, racism, and war. A world built on human solidarity. A socialist world. $12. Also in Spanish and French.

America's Revolutionary Heritage
MARXIST ESSAYS

George Novack

A materialist explanation of the American Revolution, Civil War and Radical Reconstruction, genocide against the Indians, rise of American imperialism, first wave of the fight for women's rights, and more. $23

PATHFINDERPRESS.COM

EXPAND YOUR REVOLUTIONARY LIBRARY

Are They Rich Because They're Smart?
Class, Privilege, and Learning under Capitalism
JACK BARNES

In battles forced on us by the capitalists, workers will begin to transform our attitudes toward life, work, and each other. We'll discover our worth, denied by the rulers and upper middle classes who insist they're rich because they're smart. We'll learn in struggle what we're capable of becoming. $10. Also in Spanish, French, Farsi, Arabic, Greek.

State and Revolution
V.I. LENIN

"The relation of the socialist proletarian revolution to the state is acquiring not only practical political importance," wrote V.I. Lenin just months before the October 1917 Russian Revolution. It also addresses the "most urgent problem of the day: explaining to the masses what they will have to do to free themselves from capitalist tyranny." $15

The Workers and Farmers Government
Joseph Hansen

How experiences in post–World War II revolutions in Yugoslavia, China, Algeria, and Cuba enriched communists' theoretical and practical understanding of revolutionary governments of the workers and farmers. "What is involved is governmental power," writes Hansen, "the possibility of smashing the old structure and overturning capitalism." $5

New edition!
Che Guevara on Economics and Politics in the Transition to Socialism
CARLOS TABLADA

It's essential for working people to win state power, said Ernesto Che Guevara. "Then there's the second stage, maybe more difficult than the first"—the transition from dog-eat-dog capitalism to socialism. That includes moving from work as a condition for survival, to voluntary social labor through which we express our common humanity. Includes Fidel Castro's 1987 speech "Che's Ideas are Absolutely Relevant Today." New edition with substantially expanded selections from Guevara's writings. $17. Also in Spanish, coming in French.

Women in Cuba: The Making of a Revolution within the Revolution
VILMA ESPÍN, ASELA DE LOS SANTOS, YOLANDA FERRER

The integration of women in the ranks and leadership of the Cuban Revolution was intertwined with the proletarian course of the leadership of the revolution from the start. This is the story of that revolution and how it transformed the women and men who made it. $17. Also in Spanish, Farsi, Greek.

Leon Trotsky on China

Articles and letters on the Chinese revolution of 1925–27. Trotsky records the fight to reverse the disastrous course of the Stalin-led Communist International of subordinating working people there to the leadership of the capitalist-landlord Chinese Nationalist Party (Kuomintang). $28

Pathfinder Press accessible ebooks for the blind, those with low vision, or other challenges reading print books

For a list of current accessible titles, go to: pathfinderpress.com/collections/books-for-the-blind.

Visit bookshare.org for information on how to sign up.